W9-CDZ-392

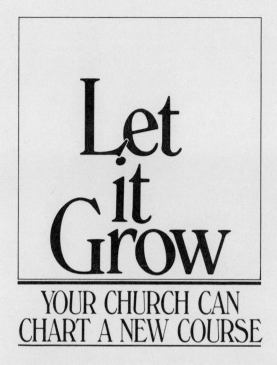

Let it Grow

YOUR CHURCH CAN CHART A NEW COURSE

MARVIN·G·RICKARD

Foreword by Tim LaHaye

MULTNOMAH PRESS
PORTLAND, OREGON 97266

Photo Credit by Russ Keller
Cover design and illustration by Larry Ulmer

LET IT GROW
© 1984 by Marvin G. Rickard
Published by Multnomah Press
Portland, Oregon 97266

Printed in the United States of America

All rights reserved. No part of this publication may be reproduced, stored in a retrieval system, or transmitted, in
any form or by any means, electronic, mechanical, photo-
copying, recording, or otherwise, without the prior written permission of the publisher.

Library of Congress Cataloging in Publication Data

Rickard, Marvin G.
    Let it grow.

    1. Los Gatos Christian Church.   2. Church growth—
Case studies.   3. Rickard, Marvin G.   I. Title.
BX9999.L683R53   1984   254'.5   84-22733
ISBN 0-88070-074-2 (pbk.)

84 85 86 87 88 89 90 – 10 9 8 7 6 5 4 3 2 1

This book is dedicated to my
faithful, loving, and capable
wife, Joyce, and to my family,
Jeff and Kris Rickard, Tim and
Julie (Rickard) Bowman, and
Doug. They have been faithful
through the many and varied
experiences and episodes of our
long ministry with one
congregation.

My thanks to Doris Schweitzer,
one of our excellent secretaries,
for typing this book.

My respect, love, and
appreciation to our wonderful
congregation and its committed
team of leaders and workers.

CONTENTS

FOREWORD

The Los Gatos Christian Church is one of the most incredible churches in America—and I am a student of Bible-preaching churches. Even when one knows just how incredible it is, you are not prepared for the spirit of love, warmth, and worship you sense while attending a service there.

The first time I conducted a Prophecy/Family Conference in that church, they had seven hundred people in attendance at two morning services. Fifteen years later they have over 5,000, not counting the 700 they gave up to start a sister church across town under the direction of their associate minister, Richard Marshall. Today, that second church is running just under 2,000! They must be doing something right.

When Marvin sent his manuscript for me to review and write this foreword, I was pressured beyond belief. "One more project," I thought. But I made the mistake of reading the first chapter and couldn't put it down. I have been writing a daily devotional guide each morning on the book of Acts to give to the supporters of our TV program, "LaHayes on Family Life." This book reads like a twentieth century version of the first century church I have been studying. As I read it, I was reminded of the expression in Acts, "and the Lord added to their number daily such as should be saved."

You may have trouble believing what you read about this great church, but it's all true. I have been there five

times; one of our daughters married a young man who had
been saved and discipled there. Ministers from all over
America and Canada visit the church and go away shak-
ing their heads in amazement.

What is the secret of this church's growth? There is no
one thing they're doing that puts it all together. They are
doing many things right. However, all the things they do,
any church or pastor could do if they're willing to pay the
price.

First and foremost it is a Bible-believing, Christ-
honoring, Spirit-filled, missionary-minded church with a
godly minister who preaches practical down-to-earth sermons that teach, inspire, and evangelize. Marvin's wife,
Joyce, has been an exemplary minister's "helpmeet" with
a gifted music talent that glorifies the Lord. They are one
couple that deserve each other. And for the record, they
are workaholics who believe their God can do anything.

In a day when many ministers have been intimidated
into silence and noninvolvement by the anti-Christian
media, it is refreshing to see such blessing on a minister
who recognizes that we should be salty Christians in a de-
caying society. One of the reasons secular humanism controls our culture and is leading it toward Sodom and
Gomorrah is because the church has lapsed into silence.
Pastor Rickard has faithfully used his influence to halt the
spread of Sodom and Gomorrah into his community. He
is one of those courageous voices who speak out against
the modern holocaust of abortion, homosexuality, por-
nography, child molestation, divorce, and the other family destroying policies. But he does more than speak out.
He prays, organizes, and marches out to city council
chambers, the state house, and every other place of influence. And he is doing the only thing that will ultimately
turn this nation back to moral sanity—he is raising up and

helping to get elected a local and national leadership committed to the traditional moral values we preach in our churches.

Yet all the time, his number one priority is "the care and feeding of a growing church." No wonder thousands attend his church. It is my prayer that many thousands of pastors, deacons, elders, and church members will read this book and realize they serve the same God. They, too, can put into practice the principles of this book and grow a dynamic church if they are willing to study, work, conceptualize, organize, and trust the living God to bless the faithful teaching of His Word.

I don't think any minister or board member should ever be the same after reading this book. I heartily recommend it.

Tim LaHaye

TO THE READER

Will the principles in this book work? If you as a church leader apply them, what will happen in your church?

After the major portion of this book was written, we had an opportunity to apply these basic principles.

Here is the story. Two fine Christian men from a city some twenty miles away recently asked if they could stop by. They were church elders very concerned for their dwindling congregation. While never numbering more than two hundred on the best of Sundays, their church had declined to about fifty people. No youth and only three or four children attended. Evening services were running in the twenty's, and plans were set to discontinue them.

Could I help? What should they do? They needed a pastor, but who would want to come? Yes, I could help, but the cure would be painful. New principles would need to be applied with which they might find uncomfortable at first. "Tell us more," they said.

I summarized just a little of what you will read in the following chapters. They nodded, interested but cautious. I said, "What do you have to lose? Your church will have to close its doors in a year unless something changes fast." They were silent but obviously in agreement.

I persuaded a young pastor from Michigan to fly out for a visit. Craig Fox understood these principles. He was noncommittal, but could see the possibilities if given a more or less free hand to apply them. With our church leaders standing ready to assist if needed, and with the help of a small core group of our members who would commit themselves to the struggling church, he and Debbie would give it a try. The Lord seemed to be in our decision.

After just ten months Sunday morning attendance grew to nearly four hundred each week, with evening attendance figures often well above three hundred! Building plans, staff needs, discipling classes, and missions conferences are the topics of leadership meetings. Gloom and discouragement have been replaced with crowds, conversions, and folding chairs for the normal overflow attendance.

Do these principles work? Only when tried!

THE RELUCTANT PREACHER BOY

"Are you Marvin Rickard?" the stranger asked. He had walked into the Cincinnati Athletic Goods Company and another clerk had pointed me out. I admitted my identity, wondering who he was and what he wanted.

As a California boy, I was a long way from home. It was now February, and rainy. My intention had been to enroll in the University of Cincinnati, but I hadn't read the fine print in the catalog. They informed me that I was an out-of-state student and therefore the costs were enormous, especially to a twenty year old who had to work his way through school.

"They told me I could find you here," the man said. I nodded and said little more than, "Well, you found me." He looked me over and took in some sort of impression of a slim six-footer dressed in slacks, white shirt, and tie. "Will you go down to Switzerland County, Indiana, next Sunday and preach for a little country church, morning and evening services?" With no hesitation my answer was a forthright, "No, I won't."

I was in my third year of Bible college, all three of them almost beyond my control. The first was for my parents, who asked each of us kids to take just one year of Bible college after high school "for a good foundation." Besides I had been asked to sing tenor in a quartet and the word was out that we would get to travel and tuition would be free.

It was a good year, singing in small churches each weekend, seeing California and Oregon. The others sang solos and gave testimonies. I wouldn't sing a solo but tried to give one testimony in a Southern California church. I got my tongue tangled, my words wouldn't come, and I sat down, red-faced.

The man introduced himself as Paul Bennett, senior student, but older and married. "If you don't accept this request, the people won't have a preacher next Sunday." I replied, "They won't have one if I accept!" He didn't smile at my humor. "Listen, I preached there for two years but resigned recently to do evangelistic work. They haven't found anyone yet and asked me to help. I have asked everyone I know. Someone told me that you might go just for one Sunday. I know that you are a third year student. You have had Homeletics I. You must have at least two sermons you could preach."

I had long dreamed of coaching high school students. Football and track were my choice. When that one year of Bible college was over, I would go on to a state college. Somehow I didn't. My friends said, "Why not go two years? The war in Korea will draw you in before you can get a degree anyway." So I stayed on with no real purpose, marking time.

The man persisted. "Charlie Stiles will take you there early Sunday morning. He preaches nearby. You'll spend the day, and he'll pick you up late that evening. Charlie said that you and he will drive down on Saturday evening, stay overnight with his fiancée's parents, and go on from there Sunday morning. What do you say? Will you go?"

When the University of Cincinnati told me the costs of enrolling, I was discouraged, to say the least. I was in Ohio with no plans. The Draft Board was demanding an update. Was I in college? Why not a third year of Bible college in the Cincinnati Bible Seminary?

"Okay, I'll do it, just for this one Sunday," I heard myself saying. When he left, I felt a little sick. I didn't want to preach. I was not at ease in front of people. Was there a Power at work in my life, a Hand that opened doors, closed doors, arranged introductions, and provided situations? Sure, I was born again, but I would be a Christian coach. I had never met one, but I would be an influence for Christ in the field of athletics.

Charlie Stiles weighed more than I did (to say it with carefully chosen words). That Saturday night I had to reach under the bed and get a grip on a handful of bed springs to keep from sliding downhill in the double bed. Every time I dropped off to sleep, my grip relaxed and I had to climb back up to the edge and try again. Finally, I just wedged my hand into the springs so tightly that it stayed there, going to sleep a little ahead of the rest of me.

I wasn't impressed when I first looked at the little white country church on that cold, rainy February day. It had a steeple and bell and an assembly room. No other buildings were nearby except two tiny ones located a discreet distance from the church. A gravel road led from the paved county road. The name of the place was Center Square, but there was neither a center nor a square, just another church a few hundred feet away, a gas pump, and an all-purpose country store.

I entered the empty building at least an hour ahead of starting time. Plain wooden pews sat vacantly looking forward. Up one step and I was on that platform. A sturdy pulpit looked benignly across the pews. Behind it two tall, ornate wooden chairs gave the little area additional dignity. A well-worn colorless carpet completed the scene. The attendance register indicated forty-three people had been there last week and forty-seven one year before that.

An immense and overpowering feeling of destiny pulled me to my knees before one of the chairs. Rain drummed steadily on the roof. I was alone, yet I wasn't by myself. My prayer was informal, "Lord, here I am, a California boy a long way from home. I am about to preach to forty or fifty farm people who raise tobacco for a money crop. I am lonesome and miserable and homesick. I want to go to college and learn to coach boys, but I don't want to preach, not today, not next Sunday, and not sometime. I need Your help to get me through this day. O my God and Father . . ." Tears came, almost surprising me. I just wept and stayed there. All at once I understood a few things. It was as though a Hand was on my shoulder. "O God," I prayed, "I think I see a little clearer. You want me to preach. You have been closing doors, opening doors, gently leading me to this very place. You want me to give up my plan and accept Yours. Well, if You have gone to this much trouble, I promise You that I am willing to follow You and I am willing to look for further signs of Your leading."

The people came, fifty-seven of them. They listened and made no comment. Most returned that evening. I preached but I don't remember my text or topic. When it was over, Dewey Ramsey said, "Would you mind waitin' outside? We want to have a little meeting." Well, it was raining outside. I really didn't want to wait out there. Of course there were those two little structures not far from the church, but I didn't want to wait in either of those! So I stayed in the little foyer with its coat hooks around the walls and its bell rope descending through the ceiling.

The rain poured down with great intensity while I paced around to keep warm. By and by, Dewey opened the door and said, "Come on back in." The people were all grinning at me. I thought they had called a meeting to tell me that I would never make it as a preacher. I knew that already and just grinned in return. Dewey said, "We want you to come back next week." I said, "I have already told you everything I know; what would I say next Sunday?" He replied, "You'll come up with something. We think you will be a fine preacher and we want you to preach for our little church." I started to lift my hands as though in defense and back away, but then I remembered my prayer of so many hours earlier, "O God, I am willing to follow Your plan."

PRINCIPLES TO PONDER

1. Nobody plus God's will equals an interesting and fulfilling future!

2

The little group numbered seven . . . six elders and me! It was my second elders' meeting, held in one of their homes. I was

CONFRONTATION WITH THE CHAIRMAN

nervous. The Los Gatos Christian Church, Los Gatos, California, had had a long history, since 1882. No minister had managed to stay longer than six years. Some had lasted all of two years!

Joyce and I, with our two very small children, had managed to get through six weeks so far. The six weeks had included fourteen days of VBS; we both taught. The Santa Clara Valley was having a heat wave that August of 1959 and temperatures had been averaging 102°. Our new home was going to be great, but all we had in front and back was dirt, very fine dirt, mixed with a million little rocks which had to be raked out and piled by the curb within six weeks if we wanted them hauled away by the contractor.

After a brief time of listening to the men visit among themselves, the elders' meeting was called to order. The chairman, retired, dignified, and direct, said, looking intently at me, "Young man, we have always had a good relationship with our minister." He paused; I nodded, thinking how many the church had gone through. "Here is how we have operated," he continued. "Every Tuesday the minister comes to my house. We sit down together and go over the events of the week that has passed, and we evaluate. Then we go over what is planned for the week to follow. Do you understand me?" All eyes were on me; I nodded again, beginning to understand. He paused, "You have been our minister for six weeks so far, and you haven't yet been to my house on Tuesday morning." He waited for my response. So did the other five elders. I had to say something, but I didn't need the gift of wisdom to figure out that my ministry was about to end, for all practical purposes . . . or begin.

I began to speak, slowly at first. "I understand that each of you elders is responsible for one or two of the major areas of our church work. You," and I pointed to one, "are in charge of Christian education, and you," I looked at another, "are to look after missions," and so I went around the room. It was growing tense and very, very quiet, but I had to finish.

Looking at the dignified gentleman who had tossed the ball to me, I said, "And you are responsible for finances, music, and nearly everything else. Here is what I plan to do. When I need to talk with one of you about missions, I will get together with that elder, at church, at my house, at his house, or over coffee at a restaurant. When it is education, I will meet with that man over there. And when it is one of your areas, I'll meet with you. But I am not going to come to your house every Tuesday or any other day to get permission to do the work of the ministry to which God has called me at Los Gatos Christian Church!" I got it all out, but my cheek was twitching out of control, my voice was squeaking, and I was cold all over.

He looked at me with a very direct gaze, right into my

eyes. I tried to return it, but could only hang on long enough to see the red appear on his neck above his collar. It moved up slowly until it seemed that the very hairs on his head were rooted in crimson. In the history of the world, I doubt if a pause was ever more pregnant!

I looked away, at my shoes, the carpet, the shoes of the elders. The meeting continued, but I have no memory of it from that point on. No further mention was made of "how we operate here." If I said anything more at all, I don't remember it.

Joyce was opening our moving boxes, a project delayed by VBS, raking rocks, and heat. One look at me and she said, "What is it? Are you all right?" I was near tears. "Don't bother to unpack any more boxes. I think we are going to be moving again." Her eyes opened wide, "What happened? What do you mean?" We sat down amid the mess. Word for word, I told the story. She didn't interrupt, just listened. When I finished, exhausted, she said, "Honey, I'm glad you said it. Someone should have said it a long time ago. God will honor it, you'll see." I wondered and hoped.

We were young, at twenty-eight and twenty-three. I had earned two bachelor's degrees by the time we were married. Nothing held me in Indiana or Ohio. I had headed home the very night of graduation, loading my little Plymouth coupe with all I owned. California was my home, the ministry my calling, the future unclear. We met in San Jose on a blind date, but not with each other. Her call to the ministry was as clear as my own. God had made her understand that she would be the wife of a minister someday. From our first date, a Halloween party, neither of us dated any other. Now we had been married for five years.

The little Los Gatos church had eighty-three members;

at least that was the number who voted. Sixty-five wanted
us; eighteen thought they should keep looking. They had
come up with four possibilities and had met with their first
three choices. One, a college professor, declined the
offer. So did their second choice. Number three couldn't
live on $105 per week, so they invited me to "try out."

On a warm June evening I had spoken for a Friday night
potluck dinner. My subject was "The Ideal Church," and
in twenty-five minutes I described the kind of church that
would meet the needs of many people and would grow.
Los Gatos Christian Church had experienced little
growth. Attendance was presently averaging 120 in Sunday school and 150 for worship. About 45 gathered faithfully on Sunday evenings.

That night in June, after the dinner and my message,
the six elders had asked me to meet with them for the first
time. They discussed my youth and wondered if I had the
maturity they needed. My wife's piano playing ability was
a real plus. Since my father was a minister and respected
by them, one of them said, "Well, as a preacher's kid, you
must have gained some experience by observing." I had.
The electric moment came when I answered what seemed
to me to be a reasonable question, especially in view of my
speech an hour or so before. "If we call you to this church
as our pastor, what size do you think the congregation
might number someday?"

As a singer in that Bible college quartet, I had visited
and sung in quite a wide range of churches. One stood out
above all the others in my mind. After our Sunday in Englewood Christian Church, Denver, Colorado, where
Sherman Miller pastored for so long, I had said to myself,
"This is truly wonderful. Lots of people attend. Young
people are everywhere. Even at 7:30 A.M. on a cold spring
day, they have a huge high school age choir for their 8:30

A.M. service. If I should ever be a minister, this is the kind of church I would try to build."

Innocently enough I answered his question, not aware that I was stumbling into the "small churches are better and purer than large churches" debate. So I began, "Well, if the church doesn't bicker and meets the needs of all types of people, I can imagine as many as 1000 people in worship on a Sunday morning." My answer, spoken out so boldly, startled me as I had never even been in a Sunday morning crowd of 1000. If I was a little embarrassed by my own remark, it was nothing compared to what happened next. One elder jumped to his feet and proclaimed to the rest of us, "If and when this church reaches 200 people, I will leave! That's as large as any local church should ever be!" That was his honest opinion. In all fairness I will have to acknowledge that when that time came, he graciously went elsewhere, to a small fellowship with almost no growth.

So with the experience of my first two elders' meetings behind me and with the encouragement of my young wife, I looked forward to the challenge of ministering to those eighty-three people.

It was never our intention to build a large church. Joyce and I had grown up in very small congregations and knew almost nothing of the way large churches function. We had no idea what the future held. All we wanted to do was reach people for Christ and be available to fit into God's plan for our lives.

PRINCIPLES TO PONDER

1. Never back away from a situation which requires standing alone on a principle.

2. If the pastor is called to lead, let him lead.

3

REMOVING THE OBSTACLES

How ow does a young couple with two very young children lead a church to change its image, to desire growth, to face the great unfinished task Christ left us, while maintaining harmony and unity?

So many church growth books flood the market. Not many ministers have the stamina or boldness of Jerry Falwell. Not many of us are excellent Bible expositors like John MacArthur. Few have the imagination and flair of Bob Schuller. Most of us aren't able to relate very well to the graphs and charts and diagrams in the church growth books.

Years ago I heard Dr. Medford Jones say, "The church is a living organism. Just remove the obstacles and it will grow because of its very nature." Since then, for the past twenty-some years, I have tried to figure out just how to remove the obstacles so that the church will truly be the church in the world.

One Sunday morning after church services were over, my wife and I lamented the lack of young couples our age. Attendance that day was about 180, but we could only count up four other young couples, and one couple wasn't yet born again. There was no Sunday school class for young couples. Did the formula for removing obstacles fit? What were the obstacles?

One look at the nursery said volumes. Our little church met in a new building on 1¼ acres. The town of Los Gatos had condemned the stately old downtown structure with its shingle siding, steeple, and interior wainscoting, built on a street corner with only curbside parking. The people had scraped together enough resources for the new church, building it themselves under the guidance of a contractor in the church.

To conserve space someone had devised cages for any babies brought by their parents. When a latch failed, our little Julie, then three months old, toppled. My wife was unhappy with the whole setup.

The next day, after the half time secretary left at noon, I decided to remove an "obstacle" to reaching young couples. Into my car went hammer, crowbar, and other tools. Joyce didn't know my plan but wondered why I had changed to work clothes. I would tell her later.

The furnishings of the nursery, in addition to the monkey cages, were two cribs, sides tied up with cloth strips to replace the broken fasteners; a play pen, one corner propped up with two old hymnals; and a few broken toys and nondescript stuffed animals. The window curtain was tacked to the plaster and provided a fine home for several spiders and their webs.

In Ephesus the church burned their occult books in the street as evidence of their new life in Christ. In Los Gatos I burned the monkey cages, cribs, and playpen to see if we could bring new life to the nursery. When I told Joyce what I had done, she immediately found a babysitter and joined me in painting the ceiling and walls with fast-drying latex. As I finished the painting, she scrubbed the asphalt tiled floor. The toys went into the garbage with the window curtain. We would wax the floor when we returned from a trip to "Babyland" in our station wagon. Opening a new account, we bought six portacribs, one playpen, some hanging mobiles, wall decorations, and some pictures. Before the next Sunday Joyce would make a new curtain, trimmed in pink and blue, and purchase an area rug. And finally, we added one more touch. We hired Mrs. Tank, a Seventh-Day Adventist, to be our first paid nursery worker. She worshiped on Saturday so was available on Sundays, and she needed a little extra income. She stayed with us for ten or eleven years.

Board meeting night came once a month. That Tuesday evening when the meeting was nearly over, I said, "Men, let's go look at the nursery." One deacon asked, "Where is it?" half in jest. They crowded in, speechless for a moment. "What in the world happened to this place?" someone said. They all looked at me. Some of them had built the monkey cages. Now they were a pile of ashes. I said, "This church has only, at the most, five young couples. Only three couples have babies so far. If we want to reach and keep young couples, something had to happen to this nursery. Joyce and I did the work. You'll get the bill for $300 the first of the month." A long silence followed. Finally one deacon broke it, "What an improvement! We should have done it a long time ago." And that seemed to be the general feeling. I breathed easier.

Next, we invited the other four couples to our home for an evening. I put it on the line. "Look, we need to reach young couples for Christ and the church. You are all we have so far, but there are hundreds of others out there. Some of them visit our church, but we have nothing for them. Now that the nursery is improved and Mrs. Tank is there, we need a Sunday school class for young couples.

Would you be willing to commit yourselves to be the beginning of that class? We'll have a Bible lesson and some social activities and some fun. When couples visit to worship, we can invite them back to visit the class. What do you say?"

Even the unsaved couple agreed, and so the Kum Double Class began, destined to outgrow every room they occupied except their eventual meeting room, the church auditorium (which hadn't yet been built). Soon the little nursery was overcrowded and an adjacent room was given the same treatment as the first. It, too, was soon crowded with portacribs and more space was needed. The "magic formula" for success proved to be as simple as removing a physical obstacle, plus a little elbow grease. Ecclesiastes 5:3 says in loose translation, "A dream comes true by a lot of hard work." Someone said, "Opportunity comes to those who wait if they work, work, work while they wait."

PRINCIPLES TO PONDER

1. "Whatever your hand finds to do, do it with all your heart."

2. "The church is a living organism. Just remove the obstacles so it can grow."

3. Attractive nurseries are a key to reaching young couples.

4

QUALITY PRODUCES QUANTITY

I had read Henrietta Mears's life story two years before attending a National Sunday School Association Convention in San Jose, California. I almost didn't get to hear her message. Fog had closed the airport. The convention committee did everything they could think of to fill the time. Announcements, books for sale, singing. Finally she came to the platform, small, glamourless, but exuding confidence. She seemingly wasn't at all flustered by her late arrival; she obviously had much to say. I listened to every word this renowned Christian educator said. It was humorous, serious, informative, and practical. Hollywood Presbyterian Church with its great Sunday school and youth ministry was known far and wide. There I sat, drinking it in. Los Gatos Christian Church's Sunday school averaged all of 150.

Now if your church is a rural church and population is limited, 150 may be a real crowd, a record attendance. But if your church is located in the vicinity of half a million people, as mine was, 150 is a disgrace. Maybe if the church is new and just getting started, 150 is respectable, but if 25,000 people live in your area and there are multitudes close enough to drive, your church is in great need of some changes.

Miss Mears mesmerized me. Everything she said, I needed to hear. The advantage of a convention and a really qualified speaker over a one-on-one interview is obvious: Those who need to hear something have to sit and listen without talking. I wonder if anyone else among the 2000 who were there remember what I remember. Of all that she said, one line stays with me: "Quality produces quantity." Since then, I have said that so many times and in so many places that occasionally I am credited with it myself. But it isn't mine, it is hers. Maybe she got it in some convention when she was twenty-eight. In any case, I have claimed it and tried to apply it. In that same convention someone else said another truth I claimed, but I'll tell you what it was in the next chapter.

Could her rule of church growth be applied to our choir? Something needed to be done. The final evidence was the antics of two little boys on the front row in church one morning. When the choir, eighteen of them, sang their "anthem," I saw the boys poke each other and then throw back their heads to imitate the warble coming from the soprano section that pierced us all. Her voice had been excellent, but the years had taken their toll. Then, too, her husband led the choir. Their motives were right and they loved the Lord and the church, especially Los Gatos Christian Church. Who would sing if they stepped down?

But how do you handle this kind of situation? A deacon came to me, "Will you go with me to see them?" And so we went. Audrey Mieir later on said, "Better to offend one (or two) than to offend the whole body." We were practicing the rule before I heard it. To make it more difficult, the choir director was the same elder who had wanted me to check in with him every week. Unfortunately, the deacon got tongue-tied after we had been invited in. At least he had arranged the timing so that the conversation was just among us three men. At first you talk about children, weather, or some event in the news, but inevitably silence falls and you have to get to the point.

"Well, we've come to talk about the choir."

"Um."

"Actually, we don't want to talk about the choir as a whole."

"I see."

With little tact and much prayer, I began. I felt like Nehemiah, when the king asked, "What is it you want?" The Bible quotes Nehemiah, "Then I prayed to the God of heaven, and I answered . . ."

"Your wife is a lovely Christian woman who once had a beautiful voice . . ." He looked a little sad but not angry. "But when she sings now, her vibrato goes past the note she is after and overlaps on either side. In fact, it stands out and sometimes overcomes the rest of the choir." He nodded slowly. "I see. What is your suggestion?"

It is best to go into one of these situations with a plan which is aimed at improving the quality so as to reach more people for Christ. However, it is easier to build an auditorium than to do what we were doing! Yet you never need auditoriums if you don't face the obstacles.

He finally opened up. "She will never step down as long as I lead the choir. I realize what you are saying. I am old and my hearing isn't as keen as it once was. I suppose the problem is bigger than I have imagined. It must have been hard to come to me and do as you have done. Thank you both for coming." I was afraid that we were about to be gently shown to the door, with no solutions proposed, but I underestimated the bigness of the man.

"Here is what I will do. It is almost summer. Let's just dismiss the choir a month early. I will announce that I am resigning. We will both step down and not return to the choir in the fall." He looked at me with almost a twinkle. "I suppose that you have someone in mind to lead the music?" Well, I had thought of that and assured him of my plan. "If Eileen Jessup leads the choir, who will play the organ?" I had that covered also and told him, "Elaine Platner." "If Elaine Platner plays the organ, who will play the piano?" "My wife," I answered, gently. "I see," he said, and stood up. "Gentlemen, thank you for your visit." He was so dignified and said only what was necessary. We shook hands. Mine was wet. His smile was warm, but sad.

Just weeks before, we had seen an ad or an article. Audrey Mieir was to be in town for a choir directors' clinic. Joyce and I went, bringing Eileen Jessup. We had heard Audrey's music on a long play album my sister owned. How do you describe music in words? All I can say is that Audrey Mieir's music moved our hearts. When I heard it, I felt like preaching. If only our new choir could use her kind of music, "anointed music."

That night almost no one came but us, a very unusual thing. When the evening was over, everyone went out rather soon. We waited to meet her and visit, to tell her our dreams, to see if we could spend a few minutes with her. That visit was destined to result in a lifetime friendship. It was a divine appointment, meant to be. She would supply us with music, her own and other music like it. In fact, she had a plan that allowed her to lead our choir, part by part, by means of the big reel to reel tapes of that time. As we learned the music, we would increase our volume and decrease her tape until we were actually singing the very music on the tape, with power!

Never will I forget "O That I Knew," the first song we

sang. (I sang tenor in the choir and then stepped over to the pulpit to preach.) We sang it the first Sunday the reorganized choir appeared. It was so moving. No more music from those stacks of traditional music books in the closet. No more choir that looked as if it practiced looking mean. No more "special numbers by the choir." From now on music was a ministry to be used and blessed of God as much as a sermon.

As they say, "There wasn't a dry eye" that Sunday morning. A new chapter had begun. The choir doubled in size immediately and lengthened their practice time. Quality had improved. Quantity had to follow.

PRINCIPLES TO PONDER

1. "Quality produces quantity."

2. "Better to offend one or two than to offend the whole church."

3. Tackle problems by speaking the truth in love.

4. Have a plan of action.

5. Heart-moving music is a key to drawing people.

ADDING 100 NEW MEMBERS EACH YEAR

"Big doors sometimes swing on little hinges." When you look back, you can often see your own hinges. I again sat in a workshop session at the National Sunday School Convention. The evening before, Henrietta Mears had influenced my ministry for the rest of my life. Now it was destined to happen again. This time it was Charles E. Blair, Pastor of Calvary Temple, Denver, Colorado. Pastor Blair was leading the workshop.

It is not to his discredit that I didn't know much about him. It was due to my own limited exposure outside of my own small circle of fellowship. The convention program stated that he had led his church from 100 people or so to their present 2000 at that time. I had just begun my Los Gatos ministry and he had reached 2000 in attendance. No doubt that is the reason forty or fifty ministers gathered to hear him. Most never will minister to 2000 people, but still, they are fascinated with a man who can. Some, unfortunately, are also quite ready to be critical of him as well.

Someone has said, and I have made it a rule, "Take advice from someone who has done what you want to do.

Take all other advice with a grain of salt." Maybe I made up this rule, at least the second part. Well, Charles E. Blair had done what I wanted to do. Not that I had any confidence in front of large crowds; I didn't. As a high school student I had to lead the flag salute and conduct student business in front of 1000 because of an office I held, but I was often nearly sick with waiting for the assembly to begin. Even today, with crowds of nearly 2000 at a time and another 70,000 watching on TV, I have sweaty, cold hands and a butterfly stomach.

What did Charles Blair say that day that motivated me? Most of what I heard I have forgotten, but one statement stands out. I couldn't refute it, and I couldn't ignore it, and I couldn't forget it. There was so much truth in it that it had to become my rule as he had made it his. It went something like this, "Any preacher worth his salt ought to be able to get two people a week to make a public decision for Christ." He went on to clarify his statement as if additional words were needed. We all shifted uncomfortably because he was getting too close. We wanted to hear of some new attendance gimmick, some cute publicity ideas, some way to get a bigger crowd. His method was too direct. Just go out from door-to-door until you find two people to lead to Christ, two people to join the church, two kids at the age of accountability who need to open their hearts to Christ. "Look," he said, as I remember it, "You are free from holding secular employment. While other men have to put in forty hours a week for their company and then do their church work, you are free all week long. Surely you can find two people a week. Even if you take a two week vacation, that leaves fifty Sundays; 50 x 2 = 100 additions a year. Just stay where you are for ten years and you'll be preaching to 1000 members."

I'm not a mathematician but I could add those numbers. He said, "All of you are preachers. How many of you had one hundred additions to your church last year?" I don't remember that any hands were raised. There were two or three churches in the Santa Clara Valley that were reaching more than one hundred a year; First Baptist Church, Calvary Baptist Church, maybe Bethel Assembly of God, but I don't think any of their staff happened to be there. In any case few, if any, hands went up. Dr. Blair didn't let up; he was driving home his point. "How many of you believe that the main purpose of the church is evangelism?" Most hands went up.

I suppose the others who didn't respond were either getting irritated or believed that discipleship is primary. I run across the philosophy that claims that discipleship results in evangelism, but it seems to me to be the other way around: Evangelism requires discipleship. If you don't evangelize, there is no one to disciple. I'm not really convinced that the word *disciple* is ever meant to be used as a verb. It is always a noun. You present the claims of Christ and when someone believes, he becomes a disciple of Jesus Christ. Then you or someone else needs to teach him scriptural truth so that he can become a mature disciple and lead others to Christ. Maybe I am making a play on words, but it seems to me that the churches which major on "discipling" everybody have very little growth by evangelism, while the churches which major on evangelism have all kinds of people to teach and to bring to maturity. Some churches are so involved in discipling that they won't even give a public invitation for people to come to Christ.

"How many of you would like to add one hundred members a year?" Charles Blair asked. My hand went up with the others. He said, "Then go out into the highways and byways this week until you have at least two. In my first years with Calvary Temple, I was often out calling in homes on Saturday. I still spend hours a week making calls. There is no better way to build a church in size than to add new members." We all laughed.

"How many of you will make a covenant with the Lord to do your very best to bring two people a week into the kingdom?" I was surprised that 99% of the men didn't seem to accept his challenge. I did.

It seemed so simple. Find two people this week who will make a public commitment next Sunday. Where to find them? That wasn't hard. We kept a guest register book in the entrance area. A high school girl carried it from visitor to visitor. "Will you sign our guest book? I'm so glad to meet you! I hope you will come back next Sunday." She obtained their names. I called on them, taking my wife with me whenever she could be free of the kids. The first thing people asked was, "Who was that darling girl who made us feel so welcome?" The next comment was, "We loved your music." Once in a while they even mentioned my sermon! From that list of names which seemed to be increasing, I made call after call, visiting and gently encouraging people to make a public commitment for Christ and His church.

I remember our very first "white collar" executive-type visitors, a whole family, IBM people. There is nothing wrong with "blue collar" workers, of course, but that was all we had in the beginning. When a church is stratified economically, ethnically, or racially, all others feel a little less than welcome. It isn't that they aren't fully welcome. It's just that one group finds it awkward to communicate with the other strata of society and after the brief handshake they turn back to those with whom they feel comfortable.

We were so excited to finally have a breakthrough that

Joyce and I looked up their name and address in the guest book and made a Sunday afternoon call on them. The same day they visited church. That very evening they joined, all four of them. The next week we had another IBM executive, a young family from a Baptist church in New York. The father of John Davidson, the entertainer, had been their pastor. We called on them one evening and found them to be quiet people who were noncommittal. Finally, I said, "We need you. You are leaders. Don't go to some other church. Join ours and help us reach others!" As we left, I asked, as I usually do, "Can I pray with you?" No one has ever refused. "Lord, lead these people into your perfect will, but Lord, make Los Gatos Christian the center of your will for their church home." They soon joined, taught a class, served on the board, drew charts to show the congregation where we might go in the future, and were used of the Lord in many ways. I found that people *wanted to be asked* to come into the church if they were Christians. Others who had visited seemed to expect someone to follow up and challenge them to receive Christ, follow in baptism, and get into the church.

Joyce and I had been visiting all the visitors but we couldn't keep up. They were coming by the dozens, from all walks of life, and from various social and racial backgrounds. People in the church said they wanted to help Joyce and me visit. We took them up on it! "Calling Club" isn't a very sophisticated or clever name for a visitation group, but we still use it and we still make hundreds of visits in homes. At first it was organized around a planned potluck with all those making visits taking turns with bringing a main course dish, butter and rolls, salad, or dessert.

We had no training program where people sit through

six weeks of "how to do it" sessions and then never do it. I believe that everyone who is born again can tell someone about it, and everyone who loves his church can tell about that. Stay away from the theological questions that have divided the church. When it comes right down to it, people aren't nearly as interested in theology as they think. People want spiritual direction. They need to be challenged to walk on higher ground. They need to come to Christ and to learn to love the brotherhood of believers.

Now we have a team of people cook a terrific meal for which we charge a couple of dollars to cover costs. Captains have their teams of callers and see that each is notified and urged to be there. Maybe Monday isn't the best night, with Monday night football and all, but if you wait for the best night, it will never come. The most important task of the church will always tend to be second to other programs. Satan and human nature will see to that. "Efficiency is doing right things; effectiveness is doing most important things," according to Derric Johnson. Calling is effective if you want to see at least two people a week come forward to make a commitment to Christ and His church.

PRINCIPLES TO PONDER

1. Listen carefully to someone who is doing what you want to do.

2. If you add two people to your membership each week, before long you will have more members than your present schedule and facilities can handle!

3. Evangelism efforts gain results, but it is easy to let other efforts push evangelism aside.

4. "Effectiveness is doing the most important things."

6

LET'S BEGIN AN EARLY SERVICE

Attendance was growing. Just the blessing of the music was enough to bring visitors back again. And many were coming into membership. The little fellowship hall which served as our auditorium was taxed to the limit when 180 came for worship. The rule of thumb which I kept hearing was that when 75% of your seats are full, you can't grow any more. We proved that to be wrong. I still see it in the church growth books, but it isn't true. People like to go where the action is. Just look at the beaches in summer. There are deserted beaches, but nearly everyone wants to jam up on the full ones. Look at the campgrounds. Go to a football game. If 25% of the seats are empty, some of the excitment is missing. I see churches which add a second worship hour when their first one is barely respectably filled. Now they have two weak worship hours and the people have little enthusiasm. It is better to jam them in. Crowd them close together. Put in extra chairs. It is electrifying to hear the ushers bringing chairs. It is a plus for growth when the song leader has to say, "We are going to need every seat today. Please move in and leave any empty seats on the aisles. We're going to have close fellowship again today. What a crowd! Now let's stand together and lift up the chorus of the wonderful hymn, 'How Great Thou Art!'; stand together and sing with power." Listen. The people love it and the roof nearly lifts off. Do you see what I am saying?

Yet there comes a time for a second service. In our case there came a time eventually for three and then four worship hours. Each had a full choir and we had to actually turn people away from the later hours. More on that in a later chapter.

The usual arguments against a second service in a smaller church barely came up in our case. "We won't see everyone," a few said. I reminded them that we had but one evening service and they see "everyone" there. (I have sometimes wondered why it is so important to "see everyone" on a Sunday morning and yet at least 50% of the members don't seem to use the same reasoning on Sunday nights!)

One piece of logic seems irrefutable; you can pass the offering plates twice if you have two services. Another argument is that it costs considerably less to use the building twice than it costs to double the floor space and seating.

I have never found it hard to preach the same sermon twice or three times or four times, when necessary. Somehow, if the lessons in it are good ones, I get excited all over again each time for the privilege of sharing them with another crowd of people. The exceptions to this are the times when something very spontaneous wells up and demands expression. Occasionally this results in only one of the crowds hearing it. But normally each session brings renewed desire to preach the Word and to seek responses at invitation time.

Need, content, and timing (which I discuss in the next chapter) are the essential elements to consider when adding a second service. When the place will hold no more people and when no new building is soon to be opened, it is obvious that the solution is not turning people away. The need for another service is apparent to all. However, if the early service is not as "good" as the traditional service, the people who attend it feel short-changed. Some will loyally attend to free up seats for newcomers, but others will drift back to the "main service" or on to other churches. The key is content so that each service is so "good" that there is no "main service" anymore.

We didn't begin with a full choir at the early service, but we soon saw how vital it was to have similar, balanced content. Thus the need resulted in a youth choir.

A memory, embedded in my heart, served as a model in my own ministry to lift the quality of our struggling early service. Several years before, while preaching in Englewood Christian Church, Denver, Colorado, for a week of meetings, I was very impressed to see the large high school choir assembling for prayer and a brief warm-up time well before dawn on a Sunday morning. It was the month of February, snow was falling lightly, and it was dark at 7:15 A.M. Even so, a tremendous number of young singers were coming to the building and assembling in the lower auditorium. That early service was well-attended, the music was excellent, and we were blessed and impressed. When the morning was over, I had to conclude that the 8:00 A.M. service was in no way a less attractive or less appealing service than the later, more traditional hour.

Our youth workers came to us well-qualified and effective. We had heard their youth choir when they served as unpaid youth workers in another church. Just before my call to them they had been dashing madly from work to church and had said, "Wouldn't it be wonderful to be free of this hassle and work full-time for the Lord?" The Lord saw our need and their expertise and brought us together.

We discovered that when you have a youth choir singing for an early service, and when those high school kids have to be there early for prayer and warm-up, parents and other family members tend to be influenced to come early! Thus our youth choir was actually the foundation for the success of the added service. Youth respond to a challenge and to high standards. I see so many churches with the philosophy that you have to use what amounts to compromising methods to reach today's young people. As I write this chapter nearly five hundred high school kids have just returned from Christian camp at Hume Lake. There were two hundred others in Sunday school who didn't get to go this year. At camp there were seventy-three first-time decisions for Christ.

The added service not only needs similar quality in the music, it also needs to have the same preacher.

An error often made is using someone for the preaching other than the regular preacher. One of two things will happen. It won't be well-attended or it will be well-attended. The implications of the former are obvious, but the implications of the latter are worse. Tension will build. Few pastors, humble servants that we are, can live well with a preaching assistant who pulls more people than we do. Barnabas handled it well, but he may have been the only one in church history to let his assistant become the senior pastor while he moved aside.

There is one more thing for you to consider if you are not convinced about adding services. I read that people tend to surround themselves with up to about seventy-five people whom they know more or less well. In a church of 75 members they know everyone. In a church of 150 one can know as many as 150. Obviously, when the church grows into the hundreds, some know lots of people while others know the average of seventy-five. It doesn't really matter how few or how many members are known to each other—Jesus didn't commission the church to go into all the world and make disciples and stop when people no longer know everybody.

Yet one of the big objections to large churches is that the members won't all know one another. I have sometimes found that to be a real advantage. Consider that in a small church, one carnal member who gets bent out of shape can get on the phone and raise all sorts of turmoil. In a large church that unruly member can contact the circle he or she knows, but can't really get the rest of the church involved.

Once you have successfully launched the second service, the church is on its way to growth, significant growth. An important milestone is about to be reached. The five hundred mark.

PRINCIPLES TO PONDER

1. Crowds draw crowds.

2. Multiple services are required by growth but do not necessarily produce growth.

3. Each worship hour must have the quality of the others.

7

SUCCESSFUL MULTIPLE SERVICES

Our first attempt at an early service was not too successful. The reason was right; we had filled our building, added extra chairs, and people were still standing in the foyer looking in. But we made the usual mistake in timing. We began in the spring because that is when attendance is strongest. Easter demanded multiple services anyway so the temptation was to begin a new service right after Easter. Unfortunately, summer comes reasonably close to Easter. Vacations begin. People take weekend trips. The early service struggled to be large enough to be satisfactory, and there were plenty of seats in the traditional hour. People asked, "Why do we need the early worship time when there are plenty of seats?"

Once you have begun having an early service it is difficult to disband and then try again later. In addition, the early risers who love to come early are vocal in their disappointment when "their" service is cancelled for lack of support. We started in the spring and then struggled through fall and winter.

Fall is the best time to begin a second service. The Sunday after Labor Day is ideal. The weather is good.

Vacations are over. School is back in session. The days are still long enough to be light early in the morning. The hardest weeks are from December 1 to February 1, but once through them and into spring, the early service will have become solid and the attendance steady. You will have filled the seats in the later service, proving the necessity of the early hour. Furthermore, you are set for the thirteen weeks of summer even though the total numbers may sag a little.

For those who are trying to find the right schedule combination due to limitations of buildings and classrooms, the following might help:

The W-SS-W Plan (Worship; Sunday School; Worship). This plan features an early worship hour, followed by Sunday school classes, followed by a second worship hour. A nursery is required at each hour for children up through kindergarten.

One disadvantage to this plan is that it may leave the auditorium unused at a prime time for Sunday worship. If the auditorium is needed and is used for a large class at the middle hour, the W-SS-W plan is excellent.

The W-SS/W-W Plan (Worship; Sunday School, Worship; Worship). With this plan no classes can be scheduled for the auditorium in order to allow the church auditorium to be used for three services of preaching.

Again, as in all plans, nurseries and children's classes must be provided at all times. If a high school choir sings for the early hour, their Sunday school classes must be scheduled for the middle hour. Nothing prevents adding adult classes or elective classes at the third hour while the third service is in progress. A college class or careers or singles can meet during the third hour also. A college choir or college/careers choir can sing for the middle and third service, but they must stay until the end and not sing and leave.

The W-SS/W-SS/W Plan (Worship; Sunday School, Worship; Sunday School, Worship). Here we are adding a second full Sunday school meeting during the third worship hour. It isn't at all difficult. Nurseries and children's classes already meet, plus an adult class or two. Maybe the college class meets this hour. Special high school or college leadership classes can be scheduled for this third hour, allowing the more advanced high schoolers to benefit from extra training while still enjoying the schedule of their group. The Denver church mentioned previously used mature high school students to fully staff the third hour children's Sunday school classes.

The SS/W-SS/W-SS/W Plan (Sunday School, Worship; Sunday School, Worship; Sunday School, Worship). If sufficient numbers of people like to rise early, the addition of adult classes or special youth classes at the early hour can utilize more good space. The disadvantage is the tendency to draw people from the worship services to the classes, weakening the early service.

We recommend keeping junior high classes at the middle hour so that families with children of all ages can find their own schedule. This is best for high school classes as well.

Hold on to your hat, now, we have one more schedule to offer which we actually used for four years!

The SS/W-SS/W-SS/W-SS/W Plan (Sunday School, Worship; Sunday School, Worship; Sunday School, Worship; Sunday School, Worship). You can actually run four worship services and four Sunday schools on a Sunday morning. If your people can be persuaded to attend either the first two hours or the second two hours, it works best.

Human nature, however, will tend to pull more people into the middle two hours, leaving the first and the fourth sessions the weakest.

When you are desperate for space and can't build fast enough, you can use this schedule for awhile. I don't recommend four years. During this time we were also in double evening services. Six church services per Sunday can wear a staff down a bit.

This plan is simply double double-services. Again youth classes must remain near the middle. Adult classes can be scheduled whenever space is available, as long as you offer a place for every member of the family at every hour.

As I remember it, for those who want specifics, the times were 8:00, 9:10, 10:20, 11:30. Just add ten minutes to each hour and you have the starting time for the next. We concluded by 12:30 each week.

No, it is not ideal. It requires considerable streamlining, but what do you do when growth is adding people faster than you can add space? You improvise. An hour is too brief, yet a service can be conducted without feeling rushed. How many separate prayers must a service contain? We cut back from five to two. Are oral announcements necessary? Does the Holy Spirit require long invitations or can people be convicted to come forward with short altar calls?

We had to use Disneyland style ropes to guide the people waiting for the next service. If they work there, why not at church? People had to exit from certain doors only; those waiting came in on the heels of those leaving, but it was exciting. We remember those hectic, crowded days with real nostalgia . . . and relief.

When the number of services grows beyond his physical ability to minister, the pastor must call on others to help. Most male staff like to preach so the task of sharing the preaching load is rather easy to accomplish. There are a few pitfalls and other things to keep in mind. The ego is a wonderful creation of God, and it drives us on to excel and to move ahead. Yet, Satan can take a little preaching time and send it right straight to a man's head. This can cause a problem in the assignments of sermons. Also, if a man has a full responsibility in another specialized field of ministry, his study and preparation time will have to be taken from that area. Additionally, when another staff person is required to preach, he has to ask others to cover the places he would have been in that hour.

In spite of the drawbacks and unknown factors, we have discovered that our best combination is to rotate other ministerial staff into regular preaching assignments, while leaving the majority of preaching to the pastor. Some churches have found a man of exactly the right temperament to add to their staff for no other purpose than to assist in the preaching and in the pastoral ministry.

With a commitment to week-by-week expository preaching through Bible books, assignments and outlines are prepared weeks in advance so that the messages at Los Gatos Christian keep their continuity no matter who is preaching. Styles vary greatly, of course, but this is mitigated by the verse-by-verse approach to Sunday morning preaching. I prepare the outlines for myself and others to use, but on those occasions when another has worked out the outline, I have not found it difficult to develop my sermon from it.

One final word on multiple services. A very consistent use of time adds much to the success of the plan. When services run late or fail to start at the announced time, the confidence of the people in their leaders is weakened.

Furthermore, if space inside the buildings or in the parking lots is critical, it is all the more reason to be punctual.

I observe that many churches need to move from a single service of praise and worship to a second. Even more churches ought to add a middle hour preaching service, thus utilizing that excellent hour to draw a crowd and to use the otherwise empty auditorium.

PRINCIPLES TO PONDER

1. Timing is as important as need and content.

2. The best schedule is the one that meets the needs of the most people.

8

TIME TO BUILD

If a church is growing, you can hold off a building program only so long. But as glamorous and exciting as it is to see a new building going up, it is a dangerous time for a church. More fights, factions, and fusses come up over buildings than over doctrine or anything else. Debates arise over which to build first, the auditorium or classrooms. The more conservative types of people worry over the possibility of a depression and that the church will "go under." They ask, "Where will the money come from?"

I'll have to admit to helping the Lord a bit in our first Los Gatos building program. When Joyce and I started, the plan was to build classrooms even though we worshiped in a fellowship hall. Plans were drawn and the church had voted to build. However, I know for a fact that the auditorium is where the people put their money in the offering. Thus, the more people you can get to attend worship, the better the income. Not that classrooms aren't important. They are, but they cost plenty and don't actually pay for themselves in the same way an auditorium does. Fortunately I had support from two groups in suggesting that we needed an auditorium more than

classrooms. One group who supported the idea wasn't sure
that we could afford to build anything and an auditorium
seemed less likely to be built than classrooms. The other
group saw the logic of what I have said about where the
money is given. The third group had worked hard to develop plans for classrooms and naturally, they hated to
have to start over.

Our best argument for an auditorium was the fact that
the fellowship hall was now jam packed twice each Sunday morning. In fact, we had even eliminated the two outside aisles by adding more folding chairs. All we had was a
center aisle. Sometimes people had to stand or sit in the
hallway. (I have been glad over the years that fire mar-
shals don't seem to work on Sundays!) Our choir covered
the platform.

Money was the biggest argument against building an
auditorium. We owned a piece of property where the original old buildings from 1882 had stood. If we could sell
that land, we would have the funds to build. Plans were
drawn for a simple laminated beam building to seat 435.
Bids were accepted. I had been beating the bushes to find
a bank that would loan to churches. It was hard then,
when we only needed $50,000. It is nearly impossible
when you need a million or two. Well, I found a bank that
would loan us the $50,000. The problem was that our new
building bid was $67,543. The lot we owned downtown
was worth about $25,000 at that time. Someone wanted
to buy it but they wanted a bargain.

This is how I helped the Lord work out our financing. I
went to that old, inscrutable bank president one day to see
if he would raise our tentative loan to $67,543. He an-
swered with no expression, "My boy, I don't really see how
your little congregation can even make the payments on
$50,000, let alone $67,543, especially at 6% interest.

(Our original loan which had to be refinanced was 3%.) He reminded me of a man-shaped computer. I could detect no feeling, no sympathy, and no desire to help. I wondered if he had a pulse and was tempted to reach across the desk to check. I was wrong. As I got up to leave and had thanked him, turning to find the way out I heard him say, "Just a minute. Please sit down." I did, and he left for a few minutes, returning with a file folder. Leafing through it he said, "I see that you have title deed to a piece of property in downtown Los Gatos. Why don't you sell it?" I told him that it was worth at least $25,000 but the only offer we had was for just $17,000 and the leading man on our board was totally against selling it for less than it was worth. With a barely discernible twinkle in his inscrutable eye, he said, "Young man, bring him in."

I managed to do so but can't remember how. If I misused the truth slightly to accomplish my plan, the Lord has mercifully erased it from my memory. I have also repented, just in case. When the three of us were seated, that old, tough bank president leaned across the desk and looked at my man and said, "So you want to build a church auditorium." My man nodded slightly, very slightly. I swallowed. "From what I see by these attendance graphs, you need one," he continued. Another very slight nod. I swallowed again. "I understand that you have an offer on that downtown property. Is that true?" My man said, "They want to steal it."

Then in a voice that sounded like sandpaper the banker said, "My friend, you need to build your auditorium. If you sell the property downtown for the amount of the offer, you can do it. If you hold out for what you think it should bring, you will lose your building bid. I guarantee that if you wait until next year to build, the increased costs will more than equal what you think you are losing on the downtown property. You can't have your cake and eat it too. Either you sell and get your building built or you look for a better offer on that lot. Which will it be? Are you in the real estate business or are you in church work?"

I nearly died. My heart was pounding. I couldn't even swallow. I think I detected the tiniest of winks as the banker looked at me, and my man looked out the window. It may have been a twitch. I'll never know for certain. Then my man spoke, "I see," he said. That was all. The ride back was a little tense with rather long silences and many short subjects of conversation, mostly by me. But that night at our board meeting my man said, "Men, we have to decide if we are in the real estate business or in church work. Even if that lot is worth $25,000, let's accept the offer of $17,000 and sign the contract on our new auditorium."

Since those early days, we have had more building projects, remodeling, and financing than I can remember. Each has been different but none has been easy. Each caused some tensions in the church, but each has enabled us to reach more people. In that first project I had to convince the people that we could meet the payments on the increased debt. This may sound a little funny, but I made a chart, attached paper money to it, and announced, "The chart with the paper money has on it the exact additional amount we will need each week to make our new payment. If you will increase your giving to help meet the need, just remove that amount of paper money. Don't sign on anything. We'll know when the chart is empty that we can meet the increased obligation." In a week or so the paper money was gone. We absorbed the additional cost so easily that we all wondered later why we had worried.

A few rules for building programs should be noted. The

debt service costs should be kept within 25% of the total budget. A church is on safe ground with that ratio. The interest rate is not the most important consideration. Usually the rate of inflation adds value to the property at least at the same percentage as the new loan. So often I have reminded our church that in Roman times the cost of going forward for Christ was human blood. We can do so today for mere money. If we wait for ideal conditions before building, we will wait too long.

Sometimes people want to start a building fund and save up so as to pay cash and avoid using the Lord's money to pay interest. That sounds good, but at the same rate the money is being set aside, inflation is adding to the cost of that building. Few churches can set aside large enough amounts to actually build free of debt. If we had tried to save money for that first building, it would have taken ten years. By then it would have cost three times as much for the same size building. Thus we would have had to borrow twice as much ten years later at much higher interest. Meanwhile, we would have been totally stifled for growth. On the other hand, because we went ahead, ten years later we were averaging 1500 for worship in three services and were ready for relocation to a 2000 seat building on thirteen acres.

As I have said, many congregations build too soon. Why build if you aren't crowded? Send money to missionaries rather than use it to simply have a finer "sanctuary."

Incidentally we quit using that word to describe the place in which we meet for worship. Even though God doesn't dwell in buildings made with hands our human tendency is to call an auditorium a "sanctuary" and a church structure "God's house." Maybe that is the reason so many church bulletins say, "If you must whisper,

whisper a prayer." That explains why the minister comes out and intones, "The Lord is in His holy temple, Let all the earth keep silence before Him." Little kids look up to see in which dark corner He is hiding. The organist seems not to have heard the part about silence and turns up the volume so that you might as well not even try to sing along anyway. The Lord, by His Spirit, dwells in each believer. Why then should it be thought unacceptable for them to talk to each other in the auditorium before time to sing or pray or preach? Personally, I love the sound of the body of believers as they greet each other, form new friendships, and make guests and visitors welcome. Surely the Lord isn't offended by the sound of the voices of His children.

Leave building as your last alternative. Double services, triple, even quadruple morning services if necessary. Your people really know that an expensive building is needed after a few months or a year or two of such a schedule!

We have tried several methods of building programs, none of them easy or necessarily best. You can't do anything much without money. The more you have, the more you can do. Not that the work of the kingdom is based on material assets. It isn't, but in our society they sure do help. I would like to mention a few methods and comment on them.

Do it yourself with volunteers. This method works, especially on simple one-story construction, but tensions always rise. After a big start and a few wonderful Saturdays, the "crew" dwindles to a faithful few. The faithful few, who have the time and are skilled, fight feelings of resentment at other men who don't come or who when they come, don't work much. What the "workers" may not know is that some who have few building skills and others who have no free time may be giving double tithes to compensate. And they can't very well announce that. Also, this method drags on too long. The momentum can be lost when the anticipated new building is obviously not going to arise overnight. Another drawback is often unavoidable and almost certain to happen. On dedication day, when all the credits are given or printed, some electrical or plumbing contractor or someone who donated a toilet, a fusebox, or ten gallons of paint will be unintentionally omitted.

Contract the project, but hold out some work for the volunteers. This is a good plan if too much isn't given to the men and women of the church to produce and as long as the contractor isn't delayed. Some people do want to participate in the actual building. This plan can save the church a small percentage of the cost by their donated time, equipment, skills, and materials. In a major project involving several stories, tilt-up cement, or unique processes, about all that can be withheld from the contract is whatever painting is not too dangerous or maybe some outside flat concrete work or landscaping.

Contract the whole project, but hold out a few separate items to hold the cost down. We have had to do this on more than one building project. I always regret it at the time. I have discovered that some of those items are never "added later." The ones that are "added later" are painful to accomplish. The problem is that other things become more important than the items left out. You are handicapped by the lack and the expensive building project is never quite as useful as it was designed to be. You just get used to the lower quality.

Contract the whole project and include everything you can think of in the contract. I like this one best. The church can go on doing the work of the Lord without interruption. Too often a building program gives people the distinct impression that when the project has been completed, the "Lord's work" is accomplished. Too much emphasis is on buildings today anyway. They are only tools to use. The building isn't the church. It may even hinder the church if it is designed too formally or too plainly. The energies of the men of the church ought to be on reaching people for Christ and then bringing each believer to maturity. Building programs offer an impressive substitute for the members' time, talents, and gifts. It is too easy to get sidetracked. The work of the church is with people, not paint. Consider how easy it is to get deacons to serve on the property committee or finance committee as opposed to education or evangelism committees. The more people-related the job is, the harder some people backpedal!

By the way, I like what I heard someone say about volunteers in church work. "Jesus isn't looking for volunteers, He is looking for servants." Paul called himself something one step further. He called himself a bond servant, even a slave.

The difference between a volunteer and a slave is awesome. In *Sold Out* Clive Calver, English evangelist, outlines three differences between our practice of selecting leaders today and that of the early church.

We look for natural ability—but they looked for an endowment of power, for men set apart by the Holy Spirit for the work of ministry. Not just men who thought that they could do the job, but men whose ministry was recognized by others. "While they were worshiping the Lord and fasting, the Holy Spirit said, 'Set apart for me Barnabas and Saul for the work to which I have called them.' So after they had fasted and prayed, they placed their hands on them and sent them off" (Acts 13:2, 3 NIV).

We look for qualifications—but they looked for spiritual maturity. Yes, of course, ability and qualifications are important, but how much more important is it for us to have spiritual leaders who are "men of good repute, full of the Spirit of wisdom?" (Acts 6:3 RSV).

We look for men with personal charisma and following—they looked for men whose lifestyles were consistent and disciplined. Men who were the same in the quietness and privacy of their own homes as they were when ministering to the people.

Let me conclude by saying that during a successful building program in a church that is unified, two things are almost inevitable. Offerings will increase and attendance will be larger than usual. So obvious is the expenditure of funds that the members increase their giving without any encouragement at all that they do so. Then too, when attendance is up, giving is usually up as well. People want to see the progress from week to week, especially after the first of the cement is poured.

I remember the day that the big wooden beams were lifted into place for our first new auditorium for 435 people. The grammar school across the street dismissed six grades so that the children could watch from the school lawn as the giant crane lifted the beams into their permanent positions. And when Sunday came, the people were drawn to the sloping cement slab under the shadow of the emerging roof structure. Finally, they could begin to visualize what the builder was doing and they were enjoying it.

Wise old Solomon said, "There is a time to laugh, a time to cry," and time to do the events of life. He knew best of all that there is also a time to build a church building!

PRINCIPLES TO PONDER

1. Debt service should not exceed 25% of the budget.

2. Don't count on hoped-for new members to meet the new debt service.

3. Saving in order to pay cash later may cost more than borrowing to build now.

4. Church workers ought to be called "workers" and "servers" rather than "volunteers."

9.

RAISING THE MONEY

I have never been a fund-raiser. I know pastors who seem to thrive on this challenge, but I am not one of them. Asking people to give more is hard for me. I don't mind telling what the needs are, and I am quite comfortable preaching on Christian stewardship, but when it comes to raising the money to build needed buildings, I feel uneasy. The part of a church service I am most likely to inadvertently omit is the offering.

Nevertheless, I have been through many building programs and one relocation project and we have always found the money to meet the need.

One time we decided to employ an outside firm which specializes in raising funds in churches. The initial cost for us to retain them was $8,000, but in view of the large amounts in the millions that would raise, their fee was very fair. I liked the plan. Our elders liked the plan, and our entire board liked the plan. So we began to work it, exactly as it had been very successfully done in many churches.

Unfortunately, I was not comfortable in the role I had to fulfill. It was a fine plan, led by committed brothers in the Lord. The time came when I had to be open with my elders and congregation. I believe that God works through the man he calls. I couldn't proceed and admitted it to the church. They cheered and even wept and we simply didn't continue. It cost us $8,000, but it was better to wait for the more clear leading of the Lord than to move where the door was not fully open.

I want to suggest a few plans for raising building funds.

Ask the congregation to cover the entire cost without borrowing a nickel. It can be done. I read of others doing it, but we never have done so at Los Gatos Christian. Think what savings on interest or what a fine facility you could build without having to give so large a sum to the bankers. Actually, every church in America could build every needed building with this plan, easily in fact.

If every new member added by transfer were a tither, and if every new believer were to give a tithe within a few months of his conversion, no church in America would have any financial crisis and every building would be built for cash. And every church would be booming in converts and numbers of people and faithful attendance because "Where your treasure is, there will your heart be also," according to a Noted Authority on such things. Our trouble is that too many modern believers are baptized in water, but their wallets and checkbooks are hanging in their clothes in the baptismal dressing room. Tithers are needed. The church is weakened today by immature Christians who spend God's part on their own pleasures. Thank God for the 20% or so in each congregation who honor and obey God with their tithe and more. No congregation in America could survive without them if it owns property and frees its leaders from secular employment.

Raise as much cash as you can and borrow the rest from a

lending institution. The main rule to follow is to keep your payments within 25% of your total expenses. As unfortunate as it may be to pay high interest and bank points, the alternative of not building is worse. The main thing is to get on with reaching people for Christ, even if it costs too much. One important principle: Never depend on expected numerical and financial growth to make the payments. No debt should be incurred that the present congregation can't handle. Some churches just haven't grown immediately as a result of adding space. Many other factors are more key to growth than facilities. The early church grew like wildfire with *no* facilities!

When obtaining a loan I have discovered that bankers don't accept "faith in God to provide" as sufficient evidence of your ability to pay. The following must be in hand upon applying:

- An up-to-date audit.
- Average weekly attendance over the previous five years.
- Your income and expenses over the previous five years.
- A copy of the Standard Form of Agreement between the owner and contractor.
- A debt service schedule.
- A copy of your latest balance sheet.
- A copy of your latest budget.
- An outline of any capital giving programs.
- Forecast data on projected membership increases and giving over the next five years.
- Demographic and geographic data on present membership; i.e., age breakdown, residential areas where membership lives, and occupational breakdown on your membership.

- A list of all church officers and their respective titles, terms of office, and occupations.

Some banks may not require all of this information but it is advisable to provide it to justify the loan commitments you are asking the lending institution to make.

Any graphs that show growth in members and finances add to your credibility. Even before formal application is made, we have found it very beneficial to invite the bankers to our offices and give them a tour of the property, introducing them to staff. They can get a feel for the life and strength of an organization just by a quick look and a visit. I have observed that many churches make application for a loan *before they are ready* and then have to go back and do their homework.

We have never obtained a loan on the strength of having a few wealthy men cosign or stand behind the church's loan. I hope we never have to. The local church is every member. The entire congregation is standing behind it, not a few wealthy members.

Borrow the money from members and friends of the church and pay them a reasonable return. I really like this plan. There are organizations in every state which help churches borrow from their members. Here is how they work. A member buys a note or many notes. Every six months an interest coupon matures which the member cashes like a check at any bank. The notes are set up to come due at intervals, specifically spelled out and agreed upon. A certain percentage come due and are paid off each year. The church absolutely must set aside funds to meet the due dates. If the notes were purchased with interest compounded, this simply results in a larger return at the date of maturity and there are no interest coupons to pay every six months. Some plans even allow young couples or others with no cash but who wish to help with the building program to put 20% down and make monthly payments. The church gets the full amount of the note to use for the building. Actually, this allows, even forces, members to set aside money for their own future, for college, future trips, or other long-range plans. A big advantage is that no "run on the bank" can jeopardize the church security. Notes are legally required to be paid off only on the date of maturity and not before. In our case we have a policy of reselling notes for members who "have to have their money" or of simply paying them off early when church funds are available. The entire congregation can participate in this plan. It seems better to pay interest to our members than to a bank. With an investment in the church, they tend to be more loyal and concerned about the entire ministry.

Hire an outside fund raising organization. We have never used this plan, but it has benefited some churches. Target dates are established. Teams are trained to ask for money from the members, beginning with the potentially large gifts. Potential big givers are put on committees and given important titles (sometimes totally regardless of spirituality, faithfulness, or lifestyle). The outside organization forces the church to make every call, beat every bush, and confront every member. The professionals are trained to be bold, aggressive, and "challenging." They don't mind telling a member what they think he should give over the next three years.

The advantages to the plan are as follows: Once the ball is rolling, as it will in a short, professional drive, the "everybody is doing something" psychology takes over. As public testimonies are given and individual amounts pledged are announced, members feel an almost irresistible compulsion to do what they can. Many give or pledge to the point of sacrifice, and that principle is sorely needed in the church today. When the campaign is over you really know who your members are! You also know which ones suddenly decided to attend elsewhere.

In a church which raises funds by pledging, this plan works best. In a church like ours where we use Dwight Moody's motto, "Trust God and tell the people," it is offensive, to say the least. I have mixed feelings. Stewardship in most churches is much lower than what it should be. I am the first to admit to sacrifice and give to the Lord's work. But the fine line between Biblical challenges to good stewardship and Madison Avenue techniques of arm-twisting is a line I don't want to step across. If people leave, it could actually be a purifying of dead wood and carnality. It could also be the loss of members who would one day come to Christian maturity.

There are other building fund plans and there are variations of these. The important thing is to build buildings so as to reach more people for Christ "while it is yet day, before the night comes when no man can work," and then to bring each one to maturity. In 2 Samuel 24:24 David says, "I don't want to offer to the Lord my God burnt offerings that have cost me nothing" (LB).

PRINCIPLES TO PONDER

1. Only build after adding multiple sessions while growing. But when the time comes to build, don't delay.

2. Don't be afraid to challenge people to give.

10

THE MIRACLE OF FINANCING

I have told the story of the "Miracle of Financing" over and over. Sometimes spontaneous applause erupts when the implications of it sink in. We had exhausted every avenue in our attempts to provide more space. We had three morning services and two evening services. We had a busing ministry. People came for Sunday school and we put them on buses and drove them to rented facilities all over the city. For a time no class of adults with the exception of our senior adults met on our acre and a quarter. And all children's classes from fourth grade up were bused off-site. The YMCA, Elks Lodge (while the high school department met in the holy of holies, our elite Training for Service kids met in the bar), the Carpenters' Union Hall, several homes in the area, and even a tent were used to gain space. Meanwhile, we bought eight adjoining acres for the purpose of expansion. Beautiful master plans of new buildings were professionally drawn. Large watercolors showed how it would look. A congregation of 2000 could be accommodated if we should grow from the present 1200.

We didn't have a chance. God had an even better plan

in mind. At that point, however, all we could see, hear, and feel was tremendous opposition. The city of Monte Sereno which had incorporated around our prune orchard was adamantly opposed to our expansion. The church had actually been there first, and for the purpose of eventual growth had chosen an unincorporated county area. Yet by the time we had strength and finances and the need for a significant building program, we were too late. They said, "No, No, NO!" We tried various approaches and appeals and public hearings, toughening us up for bigger battles as yet not even imagined.

I remember those meetings. Decent citizens came armed to the teeth with every possible argument. "We don't like your traffic, we don't like the sound of your singing, we don't like all the young people you are drawing, we don't like your plan, your plan will eliminate gophers, jack rabbits, and quail." One fine upstanding local resident screamed, "We don't need to be saved. Go someplace else with your hymns and preaching." She apparently echoed the sentiments of the overflow crowd in the town hall for they erupted in a sustained cheer and gave her a standing ovation, much to the delight of the planning director and a council of people who preferred horses to teenagers. We were beaten. The vote was unanimous, followed by wild cheering such as is usually reserved for a winning touchdown by the home team.

I felt tired, somewhat resentful, but perfectly calm. My mind raced with thoughts of relocation. My thoughts were interrupted as I stood in a circle of men from our church while they visited. A pert little redhead whose husband had helped lead the battle against us was looking up at me, standing almost against me. I said, "Oh, hi! How are you?" She glared at me as if she wanted to beat on my chest with her clenched fists. Instead she said, "How can you do it? How can you just smile and visit with your friends? You have just been given the worst defeat you will ever experience and you just stand there as if nothing has happened! I can't stand it!" And she burst into tears of rage and frustration. I said, "Well, we're all convinced that if this door is closed, God has a better one about to open. We aren't defeated at all. You'll see." All she could do was shake her head and shudder and say, "Ooooo!" as she ran away into the darkness.

Frankly, I didn't yet see any open doors on the horizon. Sensing defeat in our application for a use permit, we had been looking for property. You see, California is one of just two states in which your property may be zoned for churches and yet you may be turned down. A "use permit" is required. Battle after battle rages in California communities over use permits. Churches find it increasingly hard to just get permission to build, not to mention the normal difficulties of a building program.

A motto attributed to evangelist John Hagaii is taped to my desk. "Attempt something so impossible that unless God is in it, it is doomed to failure." Sometimes I am uncomfortable with the motto and place a book over it, but more often it reminds me that the church belongs to Christ and not me. We ought to expect miracles and ask for them.

Eventually we found a possibility for relocation to thirteen acres and the former facilities of a microwave company, 62,000 square feet of space. The company had closed down for economic reasons and had leased a portion of the buildings to a similar firm. The property was located 5½ miles from our Monte Sereno site. We wondered what percentage of our people we might lose who were already driving that far or more. After an open house during which staff and board members took groups through explaining how we might use the space, the people voted 88% in favor. I don't recall any hard feelings, just disappointment that we were considering a move so far from where we had been. No one wanted to stay in the community that had rejected our thriving church and considered tranquility more important than what we were doing. In the hearings the citizens had said, "We're not against churches, but . . ." and after the "but" would come their arguments against our church. It seems to me that the churches of America have been so benign for years that an entire generation has grown up with no memory of what an active strong church is like. It is okay if a handful attend and they are gone by noon; after all, a church building is a nice, quaint thing to have in your well-manicured community, but not growing churches. Ban them!

The property was beautiful. Its buildings had won an architectural award four years before and were like new. The place looked like a small college. The natural redwood vertical siding was weathering in lovely California style and heavy redwood timbers were framing the trellis-work covered with blue wisteria. An interior courtyard was accented by a fountain which shot fifteen feet into the air. The great tall flagpole in front was perfectly placed. Trees were mature and rich in foliage. Much parking was already included although we would need to add more. The neglected orchard and vineyard to the rear offered room enough. The whole setting was and is breathtaking in its beauty, nestled in a separate little valley, near the huge metropolitan Santa Clara Valley but not dominating a residential neighborhood nor shadowed by commercial buildings. Los Gatos Creek meanders along the roadway, shaded by huge white water oaks, madrone trees, and many live oaks, native to our part of California.

The interior of the buildings was open space that had been used for assembly work and would now lend itself to partitions for classrooms, nursery, library, and storage. The offices needed almost no change. Restrooms were on all three levels. The rear-most building was two-storied, as was the lower unit, while in between were the offices and warehouse, all single-storied. All the buildings were joined with covered corridors of adequate width with fine exposed aggregate concrete floors. Maybe the warehouse could serve as an auditorium, with some remodeling and the addition of a platform and choir area. Seating could possibly be made for almost 1000 in folding chairs. We would cut back to two morning services and one evening.

Yet, the big question was, "How can we buy it?" Even if we sold our buildings and land and raised a sacrificial sum from our members we would still be $700,000 short! Besides that, if we lost 12% of our membership, did that mean we would lose 12% of our income? If so, how could we meet the payments of 9% interest even if we could get the money? For these reasons and others, I was unable to lead with certainty. Purchasing Western Microwave seemed our best course, but was it? One day a man from my congregation came in. He was blunt and direct. He said, "Pastor, the Bible says, 'If the trumpet gives an uncertain voice, who will follow?' You are the trumpet, and in this matter of relocation, you are an uncertain voice. We don't know what to do. When will you take the lead and lead us?" His words stung, for he was right, but I didn't want to make a mistake and slow down what God was doing. I was of the opinion that we might win in court against the town of Monte Sereno if we took legal action.

Within the week it all came to a head, after we had looked for financing for eighteen months without success. Tom Moore had left a career with Boy Scouts of America to become our business manager. He had taken the lead in our search for funds, traveling from Los Gatos to Canada, Florida, New York, or wherever we might borrow $700,000. Several of us had been looking in our own area, especially Vern Meltzer, who was in real estate. Our offer of $1,550,000 had been accepted by the sellers but our time had run out due to our unsuccessful quest for funding. To our knowledge they had no other interested buyers. We were wrong.

On a Friday we received a call to Vern Meltzer that the sellers had another offer in hand, $150,000 better than ours, a cash deal. They were sorry but business was business and they wanted to inform us. Good luck in finding some other place. Vern begged for time, at least until Monday morning since we had every intention of buying it if we could come up with the money. Short silence. We had become friends with their representative. He believed in us and was impressed with what he had seen. Well, he guessed he could hold off the other offer until Monday, but how did we think we would pull it off? We had had eighteen months already . . .

Vern called me and brought me up to date. Lending institutions often close at noon on Fridays or by 3:00 P.M. We had applications in a few places that hadn't yet turned us down. We called them but their board hadn't met yet or they were still studying our records or hadn't they notified us of their refusal.

Saturday I paced the house. What was God doing? We were virtually stopped in our tracks in Monte Sereno. Los Gatos had tentatively okayed our potential plan to return to their jurisdiction and town, but now what? Most of our elders were at Mt. Hermon, a nearby Christian conference center in the beautiful redwoods of the Santa Cruz mountains, for a couples conference. I had called them so that they could pray. Now I decided to call again to talk to the chairman of our Ways & Means Committee. I had to talk to someone although I had no new ideas. I picked up our kitchen phone. No dial tone. Was the phone out of order or was someone on the line? "Hello?" A voice answered, "I am calling to speak to Pastor Rickard." I had picked up the phone just the instant before it rang. "I am Marvin Rickard." He continued, "It is my understanding that your organization is looking for funds for a building project. Is this true?" He said, "My name is Coleman. I'm calling from Los Angeles where I am visiting relatives."

"Yes," I answered. "We have been looking for $700,000 for months. If we don't find it this weekend, we won't need it at all. Our deal will fall through!"

"Tell me about it," the voice said. For the next thirty minutes I told this stranger as much as I could of our church, its struggles, its financial condition, the beautiful thirteen acres with buildings containing 62,000 square feet of space. He hardly commented, but occasional expressions or words told me that he wasn't missing anything. Joyce was listening to my side of the conversation and wondering what was going on, what the Lord might be doing, remembering my motto, "Attempt something so impossible that unless God is in it, it is doomed to failure." We were close to failure on the giant step of faith and relocation. Our competition turned out to be Monsanto Chemical Corporation.

"Why don't you come to Los Angeles this afternoon and we'll talk further?" the voice was asking. "Well, I'm certainly willing," I answered. "I wonder if I can get a seat." "A plane leaves your area at 3:25," he said. Funny how that precise time remains lodged in my conscious memory. It wasn't significant, just a detail of the story.

"I'll see if Vern Meltzer can come with me," I said. "He

has all of the details and the exact figures in his briefcase, plus our church financial statement. Where shall we meet you when we arrive? What is your phone number?"

I will never know exactly what happened, but the man gave me a phone number which I wrote down. In fact I repeated it out loud and my wife wrote it down also. "Is there a back-up number?" I asked. "No, this is the only number where I intend to be. If you can catch the plane, just call me when you arrive, and I will come to the Hollywood-Burbank airport." It was left this way.

Vern could come and dropped all his plans for that afternoon, but he would be running late due to having to go by his office for the briefcase. I went ahead and bought the tickets and waited for Vern. All at once I saw him coming. At the same time I thought of having Joyce call Mr. Coleman to tell him we were on our way. He could time his drive to the airport as we flew, having told us that he was about a forty minute drive from the airport. Joyce agreed to make the call, and so we headed to Southern California, a four hundred mile flight.

Our hopes were high. After all of our efforts and inability to find financing for our relocation, the Lord was about to supply all our needs according to His riches in glory, at the last minute.

Arriving as scheduled, we expected to be met, but no Mr. Coleman appeared. We had him paged and in that small airport terminal, which has since been enlarged, we looked eagerly for him to respond, but he didn't. "I wonder if he is tied up in traffic on the freeway," I said. Vern suggested that I dial the number to see if Joyce reached him and if he was indeed on the way. Carefully I dialed, and here is what I heard. "I am sorry, but the number you have reached is not in service at this time. Please dial again to make certain that you are dialing correctly." In great dismay I told Vern what I was getting and then tried again, more carefully. But the problem was the number. I had a wrong number.

Quickly I called home and Joyce said, "I know. By the time I had found out that the number was wrong you and Vern were on your way. What on earth will you do now?" Well, we prayed. "O Lord, we know you want us to buy that property. We know that Satan is trying to stop us. Show us how to find Mr. Coleman!" There we were four hundred miles from home in a busy little overcrowded airport terminal, looking for a Mr. Coleman who was somewhere in Los Angeles. We didn't even know his first name. And we had no phone number. It would take a miracle.

"Okay, Vern, any ideas?" "Well, it's a long shot, but maybe his relatives are also Colemans and maybe most of the phone number is correct, just transposed a little. Let's look up all the Colemans in Los Angeles and see if we can find a phone number almost like the one we have." It was worth a try. The problem was that the phone books for the communities which make up the huge metropolitan area called Los Angeles hang from a rod which is about four feet long. There must have been twenty or more phone books and literally hundreds, even thousands, of Colemans. We tried the plan, but it was obviously futile.

Once I had taken a mathematics course entitled "Permutations and Calculations." The thought occurred that maybe I could rearrange all of those seven numbers into all their possible combinations and then dial all of the numbers until I got the right one. I didn't remember that the number of possible combinations of those numbers was $7\times6\times5\times4\times3\times2\times1$! Nevertheless, I started writing and filled a page with possible numbers. Then I got some dimes and started dialing. After thirty minutes or so, I gave up the plan.

By now we were under real pressure. The last Saturday flight to our area from that airport was not too many minutes away, maybe two hours. Mr. Coleman still had to be found and his drive would be forty minutes of that remaining time. "Forty minutes!" Vern said. "Can we do anything with that?" "What do you mean?" I asked. "Well," he said, "Let's assume that the last four numbers of our incorrect phone number are correct and that the first three are messed up. Is there any way to find out which prefixes are from areas forty minutes from here?" There was. In the front of a phone book we saw a map of Los Angeles with all of the prefixes located according to their geographical location. One of them which matched the three digits of our prefix was forty minutes away from us. "Now, let's make up all of the possible combinations of the three digits of our prefix number." The possibilities were 3x2x1 or a total of six possibilities. I dialed all of them and on the sixth try, a woman answered, "No, Mr. Coleman is not here at the moment. I expect him momentarily. Who shall I say is calling?" With my heart in my throat, I said, "Did he say anything about meeting with some men from the San Jose area?" "Yes, he did," she responded. "Would you tell him that we are at the Hollywood-Burbank airport? We'll eat a sandwich while we wait for him. Thank you very much."

One hour later a man introduced himself as Mr. Coleman. After the introductions and some fresh coffee all around, we were down to business. Our plane left in an hour. We laid it all out, our hopes for the future of our church, our difficult task of finding financing, the extreme urgency of our need, the fact that we only had until Monday. Five minutes before we had to leave, we stood up and Mr. Coleman said, "Gentlemen, I will loan you the money for your project. If one of you will drive to a certain address in Hayward Monday morning at 10:00, I will have a letter prepared assuring you and your seller that I will finance the purchase." We had attempted something so impossible that unless God was in it, it was doomed to failure.

I built my sermon around this wonderful adventure and experience, discarding my prepared notes, and that next day the congregation rejoiced together for the definite and clear direction we had been given.

PRINCIPLES TO PONDER

1. In the Lord's work "defeat" may be the beginning of an open door.

2. "Attempt something so impossible that unless God is in it, it is doomed to failure."

3. Relocation may be best for a church.

11

INTO THE PUBLIC EYE

When a congregation first begins to grow, most of the awareness of this fact is contained within the local church and the churches with which it shares fellowship. But as a church grows larger than a community expects it to, it becomes an object of half-veiled concern. What it does may be newsworthy. What its pastor says or writes may be newsworthy also.

If I might speculate a little on this phenomena, the cause of the secular concern may well be fear. They understand and accept the fact that politicians will speak out. Leading citizens in the community may say something or take some stand which catches the attention of the media. Sports figures, educators, and heads of organizations are not likely to surprise anyone. But when a church leader emerges from the usual church-world obscurity to stand for something, there is a tendency by the media to report it tongue-in-cheek or to oppose it or to knock the church person back into the fringes where he is supposed to mind his own business.

I learned much from my first experience with the press. Before our relocation the church had grown steadily and this growth continued. For several years Audrey Mieir conducted "Sing-alongs" in our building which were open to all churches. We featured singers, choirs, instrumentalists, and just enjoyed gospel music together. These monthly events drew large crowds. Our traffic and the sound of music from open windows in the summer let the neighborhood know we were in business. Then too, the public hearings for permission to build on our land brought us into rather unfriendly conflict with many, including nearly all of the elected and salaried officials. None of the hearings made the TV news, however.

Having attended eight sessions of what was called "The Valley Forum," my wife and I were taught the basics of the Communist conspiracy and design for world control. I wasn't a "right wing extremist;" I was just a preacher. But when I saw in the papers that a certain known communist was scheduled to give a series of lectures at San Jose State University, I was unhappy enough to run a little article about it in our church paper, *The Newsette*. Our total circulation was two hundred, the minimum needed to qualify for third class mail. Somehow a local TV station read it and called for an "interview." All I had said was something to the effect that our tax dollars to provide students with a state university were now being used to teach a totalitarian view which was directly against our national interests. In a small way I was protesting.

The reporter came to my office, and his TV cameraman stood on a chair to aim down at me. The effect was a little like I was under interrogation by the authorities for doing something wrong. I defended my position, reaffirming my dismay that a communist was lecturing on a state college campus. On the six o'clock news segments of my remarks were presented with the newsman's final word, "In our opinion we conclude that ministers such as the Reverend

Rickard are far more dangerous to society than the communist lecturer." And thus I learned the lesson that the secular press is basically antagonistic to the message of the cross and seldom will fairly represent it.

This was to be a valuable lesson. I had to learn to make every word count when being interviewed by the news media and to select my own camera angles and even my own questions at times. I learned that healthy caution was always in order, no matter how disarming the interviewer seemed to be. And I learned that a grim-faced minister looks terrible on TV and that it is possible to smile even when very serious.

When a church grows larger than average, unusual opportunities often come about such as in the following account.

When Saigon fell at the close of our nation's involvement in Vietnam, little could we dream that our church would be called upon to help.

At 4:00 A.M. on April 22, 1975, five big buses rolled up the church roadway. One by one they pulled into place and their passengers alighted, carrying little bags and suitcases of their belongings. They had been traveling for twenty-nine hours, leaving the steamy confusion of Saigon and finally arriving at Los Gatos Christian Church, California, in the wee hours of a cooler than normal day. We welcomed them with hot tea and other refreshments, but most were too tired and numb to really care.

How did 156 Vietnamese refugees happen to spend a week at our church and become close friends with many of our people? When orphans were being evacuated to the Army Presidio in San Francisco, many of the women from the church drove up to help as it was about one hour's drive and calls had been publicized for volunteers. The nursery director at the church was among those who helped. She quickly observed that our own church facilities would easily handle up to one hundred babies. After receiving a word of approval and encouragement she began to mobilize our doctors, nurses, and other workers, as well as assembling any equipment we might need. A returned missionary from Vietnam made himself available as an interpreter. We were ready, but no babies were sent to us. Needless to say, our people were a little disappointed.

One week later the call came, "Could you house and care for a plane load of refugees immediately?" Our elders were meeting when the call came and prayerfully responded according to Matthew 25:35, "For I was hungry and you gave me something to eat, I was thirsty and you gave me something to drink, I was a stranger and you invited me in" (NIV). People worked all night to get ready, bringing mattresses, sleeping bags, foam pads, blankets, and pillows. We were ready by 3:00 A.M. and met for a time of prayer, asking the Lord to use us for His glory and to give us agape love equal to the hours ahead.

Security was required as these adults, youth, children, and a few older folks were the first contingency of adult Vietnamese and family groups to arrive. Their privacy and safety had to be protected. A number of police officers who are members of our church organized this important detail. This was staffed for twenty-four hours a day. Several carloads of curiosity seekers were turned away during the week.

A dispensary was set up, also staffed constantly by doctors and nurses. Two children had fevers which went away without incident, and no adults were sick at all. We treated some skinned knees and elbows and dispensed a few aspirins, sleeping pills, and other items.

Few slept much the first night as dawn was breaking by the time they got settled into their quarters. Since ours is a large facility, we housed the little families in a youth area, a carpeted, attractive place. With partitions, tables, chairs, radio and TV, magazines, and books (for those who understood or read English), it was made quite comfortable.

Our restrooms and other areas had new signs taped on the doors in Vietnamese. The Vietnamese women soon made themselves available to help cook. We bought food according to their requests (rice, ham, pork, fish sauce, tea, bananas, oranges), and they and our church women prepared lovely, tasty menus.

Many of our people took vacation time or leaves of absence from their jobs to be on hand and were of tremendous help in the whole project. Quite a number of our high school and college students took time off from school to help and in the process made lasting friendships with the Vietnamese youth. Children of our workers enjoyed playing with their little children and found ways to communicate. An inner courtyard allowed our guests to be outdoors, yet maintain their privacy, and gave the children a place to play.

We quickly became acquainted by name and began to share our faith in Christ with those who would listen. Sixteen responded, inviting by faith the Lord into their hearts and lives. In the next day or two they were baptised in the outdoor fountain in the courtyard.

A number of professional people were among those we helped, including a doctor, lawyer, banker, druggist, businessmen, and a tailor shop owner. Most were Catholic, Buddhist, or had no religion. When Sunday came we provided transportation to take those who wished to go to a nearby Catholic Church, at their request. This seemed a little uncomfortable to us, but had the situation been reversed, we would have asked to find a place of worship to our liking. Since we have three morning preaching services, about forty Vietnamese, including some who were Catholics and some who were Buddhists, came to our early service. They were very attentive and were warmly welcomed by our people.

During that week our choirs rehearsed on Tuesday, so we invited our guests to join us in the auditorium where we presented a special program. They were very appreciative and invited us to join them for a Vietnamese musical program the next night. What an enjoyable experience it was. Children sang, a number of their youth sang several songs in Vietnamese, and a top popular singer in their group sang in French, English, and Vietnamese. Most moving was their national song, "Vietnam, Vietnam." As they sang, my wife nudged me and whispered, "Look at Mr. Bach." We could see him in the back row, his head bowed, tears streaming down his face, unable to join the others in singing. It struck me then, if it had somehow failed to before, the awful tragedy of our times, the evil of Communism, and the plight of the refugees of the world. More than ever I determined to serve Christ with greater dedication, to somehow get His message to our nation and to the world, to pray for revival, and to realize that it is first of all our love which must be extended before our message can be heard—in any culture.

Since the war in Vietnam was not a popular war, to say the least, the involvement of our church with the first contingency of adult and family refugees, drew the media like flies. And they were about as pesky. They had no respect for the privacy of our guests and demanded interviews with them.

Those Vietnamese who spoke English let us know that

if they identified themselves or allowed pictures to be taken, relatives at home might be endangered. We believed them and, under great stress, protected them from the press.

When our friends left on a Sunday evening between our two evening services, tears of parting flowed and many a warm handclasp or hug of affection was exchanged. As their buses pulled out, they sang a Vietnamese rendition of "Auld Lang Syne." What a rich blessing that week had been!

It was during this time and a little before that we as a church had to go through a trial of a different nature. The public hearings in Monte Sereno were only a prelude to many more, few of them easy. Assured by an official in the town of Los Gatos that he saw no reason why we shouldn't purchase the Western Microwave property and begin to use it after some remodeling, we bought it and intended to develop it. Unfortunately, the official moved on to another community before we could finish our master plan and present it.

We were operating without a valid use permit, although officials had assured us that it would be granted. Unknown to us neighbors within a two-mile radius had been circulating petitions, counting cars, and watching us carefully. The facility had been built there with little or no opposition. Had the business been successful, its plan was to run three eight-hour shifts of workers every twenty-four hours! It would have been a beehive of cars, delivery trucks, and traffic. Los Gatos Christian Church made it the beehive of activity it had been designed to be, although we weren't having classes or services twenty-four hours a day.

Some in opposition wanted us to be a quiet little neighborhood church. They did not realize that a quiet little church could never have bought the property in the first place! Others longed for the tranquility of years past when the area was meadows and vineyards. We sympathized but defended ourselves. The buildings were there and were for sale, and we bought them with assurances of a use permit. Work on expanding parking was stopped. For months the people parked on dirt and gravel.

On the first Sunday, attendance increased by several hundred. One of our members bulldozed parking spaces as the cars were overflowing the paved areas. Now all progress came to a halt while we battled for our very existence and future. Sessions were often noisy and heated, lasting until close to midnight. Well-financed and organized, the neighborhood people issued bumper stickers: "SUPPORT A.M.E.N." A.M.E.N. was defined in smaller letters to mean "Against Massive Environmental Nuisance." That was us! They wanted to prove that we, with our youth work, our help to Vietnamese, our stand for the principles of scripture were actually a public nuisance, detrimental to the health, welfare, and safety of the citizens of Los Gatos. The public hearings of the past were children's games compared to this. On and on they went, twenty-seven of them, with fees and studies required of us that amounted to over $100,000. Meanwhile, we couldn't finish the parking nor do other work which was needed.

The newspapers reported on the conflict, not quite sure what to think of our church. Interviews were granted to TV reporters. By then we had learned to keep our comments short and to say whatever would honor Christ on TV. Surprisingly, the church seemed to flourish better when under attack than it had done with smooth sailing. People actually came "to see the church that had aroused such opposition," filling each service and all the classes until we were forced to hold four services each Sunday morning with two each Sunday evening.

Eventually, permits were granted, with heavy requirements for landscaping and architectural beauty. As attendances climbed to 3000 each week, we were no longer
the little neighborhood chapel. One vehement woman
shouted, "You are a regional church!" She was accurate.
We were becoming a church known in the whole region
and deeply concerned for the regions beyond.

Someone has said, "You can tell how hard you are hit-
ting Satan by the force of the blow you receive in return."
Church growth is an intrusion into territory formally held
by the enemy. It need not be a surprise to church leaders
when opposition comes. If a church fails to grow, it will
blend into the community like a public library, where silent people come and go but never in large numbers.

It is vital that when their churches begin to grow
church leaders and pastors be prepared for similar experiences to the three I have related in this chapter. Suddenly
the local church is in the news. What its pastor says is
being noted. It is an opportunity to lift up Christ.

Jesus said that we are to be like a city set on a hill or a
lamp on a stand. We must not be surprised at the results
when this happens.

PRINCIPLES TO PONDER

1. Church growth brings opposition.

2. Church growth brings unique opportunities.

3. Opposition from outside brings church growth.

12.

REPROVING THE WORKS OF DARKNESS

The Mercury News announced that the San Jose city council was proposing Gay Pride Week. A vote would be taken soon. The changing moral standards had given such boldness to homosexuals that they were seeking public approval of their lifestyle, a style of living once called wicked and evil and licentious. The Human Relations Commission, an appointed group, was active in the whole episode. One of its members was said to be a gay person. Most, if not all, of the other members were sympathetic.

Somehow I was invited to attend a meeting of the Human Relations Commission to "express your views on homosexuality." I assumed that they wanted spiritual direction, and since our church was now a large leading church in the area, I might be helpful in reaffirming traditional values. How naive I was. They listened intently and some took notes as I gave the biblical view. I think I remember seeing a tape recorder. Later I wished I had brought one myself. When I finished, the attack was unanimous, and it included a minister and an ex-priest. They were prepared to answer every argument and defend homosexuality from every humanistic perspective. I stood by the Bible and kept my anger under control. Not a single person on that commission held traditional American and biblical views. I say "American and biblical" because our nation's laws and moral standards were once all based on biblical commands and principles. As the tenets of secular humanism have formed our educational philosophy since John Dewey, atheism, evolution, and situation ethics have insinuated themselves into society. Where good people have not been taught the Bible as the Word of God, their thinking and their decisions have allowed such contradictions as Gay Pride. That a community should officially proclaim pride in sin was incredible evidence of the shift in moral values.

What had happened? Was it somehow the fault of the churches? Sociological changes since World War II were involved. Prior to that war, communities were fairly static and changed slowly. The war caused building booms, especially in California communities. People were moving in by the thousands, drawn by defense work or displaced by military service. As mechanization made farm work possible by fewer and fewer people, a move to the cities followed. Urbanization drew people to the cities by multitudes. Suburban housing needs resulted in acres of tract homes.

How did this rather sudden change affect churches? Prior to World War II, the influential churches in the cities were nearly all downtown. They were influential because they were large, and for another reason as well: Their ministers and pastors stayed a long time, often for twenty or thirty years. This meant stability. Their facilities were prestigious and made of granite or stone. Furthermore, the people were taught the Bible and held it up as the Word of God. Those honorable ministers were looked up to as the voice of godliness in the communities.

When they spoke out on a subject, what they said was news. Sometimes whole messages were reported in the papers, or a summary was given.

Two factors combined to weaken the voice of the church in the community. Liberalism had come into the seminaries of the major denominations, questioning the accuracy and the authority of the Bible. And the size of the old line denominational downtown churches was dwindling. Thus we had the formerly influential churches getting smaller and smaller with less and less to say to their communities on moral and biblical behavior. With no confidence in the Bible, those liberal ministers emphasized social concerns, quoting Jesus or using scripture to support their causes, but not as the final authoritative Word of God.

As the downtown areas of the large cities deteriorated, churches sold out and relocated to where the people were moving. In the suburbs they struggled to translate worn assets in declining areas into property and buildings. They required smaller facilities and could only afford modest styles. Thus the prestige and influence of the pre-World War II churches, pastored by men who preached the Bible as the inspired Word of God, were replaced by neighborhood churches in smaller facilities whose leaders majored on political issues or social concerns. Unfortunately, the position the National Council of Churches' affiliates took was often inconsistent with traditional and fundamental biblical positions.

Meanwhile, the more fundamental churches were also leaving downtown for the suburbs and building even more modest church facilities. I don't mean to imply that there were no large influential churches in downtown areas which continued to preach the Bible as the Word of God. There were, but their size and influence also decreased by the time they managed to salvage some assets and relocate.

For several years the two kinds of churches continued to hold services, to grow, to upgrade their facilities and to be generally accepted in their neighborhoods. But fundamental churches grew more than their liberal counterparts whose once-powerful denominations were steadily losing members. All at once it seemed that we heard of church after church, all across the country, which mushroomed into huge congregations in impressive buildings on several acres.

Where most churches had managed to maintain a minister, an assistant minister, a secretary and a custodian, the super-churches had youth ministers, music staff, children's workers, and maybe even a cook. Some had their own print room and printer. Moreover, a few had begun to pioneer Christian television. And some were sending missionaries out, totally supported by local churches.

Communities just weren't prepared for the sudden emergence of such churches with their traffic, their schools, their TV, their visibility, and their building applications. A generation had grown up thinking that churches were modest in size and worshiped in subdued tones in quiet neighborhoods, were dark on Sunday nights and empty all week long! And they certainly weren't prepared for the new variety of churches to speak up against anything on the basis of the Word of God and biblical righteousness.

They were largely unprepared by previous experience to deal with churches and ministers who came to city council meetings to stand against them, opposing elected officials on issues such as Gay Pride Week. The modern politician seems largely ignorant of the role of the churches in American communities throughout our history. These present politicians, other than the increasing number who come from our ranks, think of the churches as those little groups in the suburbs with their routines of worship whose leaders never rock the political boat.

With sufficient opposition from our church and others, the politicians decided it would be better to declare the special week Human Rights Week.

The Human Relations Commission was incensed and determined to forge ahead with even bigger plans. The homosexual movement is nationwide and organized to gain attention and acceptance, with San Francisco being their prize city. There were no downtown churches in San Francisco to even raise a warning voice. No spiritual revival has ever happened in that place. The natural beauty God created and man appreciates is today obscured by the incredible human sin tolerated there by the officials and the people. And many in San Jose and Santa Clara County wanted our area to be the next showplace of sexual perversion.

Thus, a proposition was introduced to the supervisors of Santa Clara County which would protect homosexuals from discrimination in housing and jobs. Believing that existing laws fully protect citizens against discrimination of all varieties and recognizing the proposition for what it was, a thinly disguised means of once again promoting and flaunting homosexuality before the people in order to gain acceptance and tolerance, we went into action.

Along with other church leaders and a group called Concerned Citizens, we began attending the supervisors' meetings to object. In meeting after meeting where public testimony was heard, no evidence was ever presented to prove the need for such an ordinance. Over twenty-four total hours of testimony was heard, twenty-three of it against the proposed ordinance. It was evident that the supervisors, with the exception of the chairman, were deaf to all that we said. Some supervisors showed their disdain for public opinion when it wasn't shared by themselves by visiting with each other when we were speaking or simply turning their swivel chairs so that we looked and spoke to the backs of their heads!

Eventually the day came for a vote to be taken. We had urged our members to attend the hearing, even providing church buses. Other churches did the same. As many as 1000 people overflowed the large board room, filling the wide interior corridors and spilling over to the outside where speakers were hastily set up. My wife and I, along with our married children, and son, Doug, were amazed at the size of the crowd. Two leading ministers saw us coming toward the building and came to meet us. "Will you be our spokesman?" they asked. I hesitated and they insisted, assuring us that places for us had been reserved on the front row.

A little additional testimony was allowed, with nothing new or different being added. The atmosphere was crackling with tension and frustration on the side of the Bible believers. The chairman of the board of supervisors asked me by name to come to the podium and express once again the reasons for our objections to the proposed ordinance. TV cameras were everywhere, as before. Just as I started to speak on behalf of biblical morality and righteousness, a most unusual thing happened. It took just a moment to realize what it was, but as I was speaking a powerful California earthquake rolled across the Santa Clara Valley, rocking that building and all within it for several minutes.

Hundreds of Christians stood to their feet and began to applaud! Then they began to laugh and cheer, breaking into song after song. I remember the ashen, sober faces of the supervisors. The drama of it didn't escape them, but they were resolute, except for the chairman, to reject the Bible and the God who controls earthquakes. To them it was coincidence. To us it was Providence.

When the earthquake ceased and subsided to little aftershocks, I said, "You supervisors may wonder why we all laughed and cheered when the earthquake hit. We are students of the Bible, and we know that many times in scripture God demonstrated His presence and ultimate authority on earth by sending an earthquake. We believe that He wants to show you that His Word is still true regarding homosexual sin." At that, the place erupted in a great standing ovation to God and the Bible, many people pointing heavenward.

When everyone finally sat down again with the steady rapping of the gavel, I spoke once more. "We urge you to reject the proposed ordinance, but if you should vote as you have indicated you intend to, I guarantee we will solicit the required names on petitions to place the issue on the ballot of a special election for all the people. And we will vote it out!"

As one, the people again rose to their feet applauding and cheering. Again the gavel rapped for order and quiet. Something in me welled up into one more statement. "Mr. Chairman," I said, "If you vote for this ordinance which has the effect of accepting homosexual practices as normal and good, we Christians serve you notice that, one by one, we intend to vote you right out of office!" I can't describe the incredible roar of approval by those hundreds of Christians.

The churches were once again fulfilling their proper role as salt and light in the community. Salt to retard the spoilage and light to illuminate the darkness of perversion before the entire community. As in days long past, the churches and pastors were the conscience of the community. We had broken out of our steepled boxes to remind the populous of the will of God. Our phone lines were nearly melted by the obscene calls we received from anguished homosexuals and others. For several weeks our home phone rang often during the night, but it was always either silent when we answered or alive with filth.

The city of San Jose, not to be outdone, passed their own version of the ordinance over our protest in public hearings. They debated less and passed on it before much could be done.

In brief, sufficient signatures in both the county and the city were quickly obtained, many churches realizing that this was no political issue but a test of conviction. When the issue appeared on the ballots, the voters rejected the ordinances in both cases by overwhelming numbers. It was evident that the community at large was willing to listen to the voice of the Bible believing churches.

Not many of us seek to be controversial or enjoy that role if it should fall our lot. Yet if only one sentry is awake on the wall when the enemy is set to attack, he had better sound the alarm. With the rise of secular humanism and the decline of our former Judaic-Christian heritage in America, we have to face the fact that other battles lie ahead. We don't want to get the church involved in partisan or personal politics, but when a moral matter ends up on the ballot, we can be thankful that we still have political means of responding. The church will have to "mix politics and religion" at such times.

PRINCIPLES TO PONDER

1. The church should be the conscience of the community.

2. "Beware when all men speak well of you."

3. Large churches can exert great influence in their communities on issues of a moral nature.

4. Religion and politics must sometimes mix.

13

VERSE-BY-VERSE PREACHING

Because God has blessed Los Gatos Christian Church abundantly, people want to know why. I can't give a good answer, for we have had no greater talent nor opportunity than many other churches. Maybe the best answer is that it is the sovereign will of God regardless of our human effort or in spite of our work and plans.

Still, I know what one key ingredient is. My people have urged me to include it. I always mention it whenever I speak on church leadership and church growth. Surprisingly, as vital as I think this part is, a great many preachers do not share my enthusiasm and tend to discount the importance of verse-by-verse preaching, or expository preaching. It is number one in our priorities of important things.

My own experience with this manner of preaching goes back many years to the day I went to see a Bible college professor named Ralph Holcomb. "Ralph," I asked, "We have had many new members added to L.G.C.C. in the past several months. What shall I preach so as to minister to them while not neglecting the others?" I had in mind that he would suggest a series entitled "Holy Spirit" or the

"Body of Christ" or the "Life of Christ" or "Ten Steps to Spiritual Growth." Maybe he even had a source for the preparation of such messages.

I did not expect his answer. "Why don't you take a Bible book and preach through it verse by verse?" I was silent, not receptive. "Get a simple outline from a few verses and then teach the material, applying it to present needs." He could see that I wasn't jumping up and down with enthusiasm. I nodded, expressionless. It sounded like hard work for a person who doesn't happen to be studious by nature. I wasn't sure that I could do it. And I was afraid of boring people to tears. He wouldn't let up; after all, I had come in to ask his advice. "Marv, you'll feed all of the people all of the time. Sometimes it will suit those more mature in the faith. Other times it will be just right for new believers. The Holy Spirit will take such preaching and make it come alive in the hearts of the people!"

I saw his point. "Where would I begin? Which Bible book?" With no hesitation Ralph Holcomb answered, "Ephesians. That is the one you should choose." I went to the Christian book store to see what helpful material I could find. Watchman Nee's *Sit, Walk, Stand* was good. Dr. Harry Ironside had a book of his sermons, *In the Heavenlies,* and William Barclay had a little book with a section in it on Ephesians. I already had *The Glorious Church* by Wilbur Fields. I "covered" Ephesians in twelve weeks, two sermons per chapter. Hardly an in-depth effort, but it was a beginning.

People began to comment. "I was blessed by the message." "I am enjoying Ephesians." "I am eager for next Sunday to come as I have questions about the next section." "I wish I had brought a notebook." "Which book will we study next?" And the attendance climbed steadily—400, 700, 1000, 1200! Growth in lives was evident, too, not because of my preaching, but at least assisted somewhat by the preaching and exhortation. Evangelism continued to be my burden. Somehow I discovered that there is no text for a sermon that does not lend itself to inviting people to Christ. Never have I had a moment's struggle in closing with an appeal for souls. Interestingly, the number responding increased as the church grew!

As I looked around in the church world I found several preachers who were doing as I was. Usually they were experiencing numerical growth in their churches. Some were becoming well-known for their verse-by-verse teaching-preaching. Many others stayed with themes and topics and God blessed them as well. But for me, I loved it and became committed to this manner of preaching the Word. I found ten advantages:

1. It builds knowledge of the Word in the people.
2. It has continuity from Sunday to Sunday.
3. It develops consistency from week to week.
4. It fills a great void in modern preaching, that is, the absence of a verse-by-verse approach in most pulpits.
5. It feeds the people, whatever their level.
6. It eventually covers every important subject.
7. It eventually covers every doctrine.
8. It disciplines the preacher!
   - to study ahead
   - to deal with difficult passages
   - to keep him off of "hobby horse" themes
9. It converts the lost and brings in a harvest.
10. It increases church income! (No one can criticize the preacher for dealing with stewardship responsibility when it is obvious to all that stewardship is the subject of the verses considered that Sunday!)

Few churches these days fill their buildings on Sunday evenings. Many fundamental churches have more empty seats than occupied ones. Most liberal churches are dark on Sunday nights and have been for a generation. Yet expository preaching can help to pack the auditorium. Admittedly, Revelation is not the easiest book to preach from but it is in the Word. A blessing is promised to those who study it. For a solid year of Sunday night services, I preached verse by verse through this book of prophecy. Sunday evening attendance averaged 2500. It was during this year that we began Crossroads Bible Church. Rich Marshall, their pastor from our staff, simply continued the messages in their rented gymnasium, with several hundred attending. More recently I announced a new series for Sunday nights through the Book of Daniel. Again attendance was large and consistent through the several months needed to complete the study.

One Sunday morning series which took all the Sundays for an entire year was a verse by verse study of the Sermon on the Mount. Incidentally or providentially, the crisis over homosexuality and the ordinances which favored special treatment and acceptance came right after the studies on "Ye Are the Salt of the Earth," and "Ye Are the Light of the World." As salt and light, the people took their stand.

When summer and vacations come continuity is lost in verse-by-verse studies, yet some kinds of Bible exposition lend themselves well to summer. A study of some of the Proverbs, some of the Psalms or the thirteenth chapter of Matthew with its parables can follow the verse by verse preaching plan with every message standing alone.

I'm a firm believer in expository preaching. Let me add one more point. A side benefit to the congregation is the fact that preaching through Bible books tends to keep the preacher from accepting invitations which take him from his pulpit. An interrupted series quickly loses momentum and continuity. Once broken, it is hard to regain. It is better to stay at home and preach.

PRINCIPLES TO PONDER

1. "Faithfulness in giving the best has big long-range results."

2. Fervent verse-by-verse preaching builds the church.

14

STAFFING A CHURCH

A question often asked ministers of large, multiple-staff churches is, "What is the best order of adding staff?" Others want to know if a Christian education minister should precede a youth minister, or if a children's worker is better for a church than a music minister, and what about an administrator?

Coming from a membership of 83 all the way to 6500 members at present, we have had lots of experience adding staff. A businessman was asked how he became successful. He said, "Good decisions." The questioner persisted, "But how did you learn to make good decisions?" The crusty, old fellow answered, "Experience." One more question followed, "Well, how did you get the experience?" The answer: "Bad decisions."

Actually, we have fared remarkably well in our choices, with many of our staff staying with us for ten years or more and few leaving in less than four years. We have never developed a chart or priority list of the ideal order of staff growth.

I have analyzed this area of our ministry and in other

large churches, and have decided that ministerial staff are added for four reasons.

Reason one: Your church has grown so that lay people no longer have the time and possibly the ability to effectively lead a particular department. Someone is needed who is freed from secular employment to work in the ministry full time. Often the very man or woman who has been so effective in lay leadership ought to be that new staff person. Several times we have seen ministries thrive so well under key lay leadership that the best solution is to hire that person. "On the job training" is the term industry uses. Why not in the churches? Bible college is the traditional way, but a family man with established financial obligations often finds it impossible to go off for the traditional education. If he is good at his Christian work and leadership, why not free him up to do more of it? Disciple him or her in the Word as time goes on.

Of course the usual method is to look for an educated, trained expert, and the Bible colleges and seminaries are doing a great work in producing potential leaders. I have discovered no easy method for finding staff. You write letters to ministers, colleges, and individuals who might know someone and pray the Lord of the harvest to send you a laborer.

Reason two: You want to begin a ministry not now being done very well. You or other leaders have a vision of what it could be but isn't. You dream of victories where few are being won. You know the key is leadership. If you can find the leader and turn that person loose to fulfill the dream, wonderful things can happen. It is essential that the person called have the same dream and vision. Otherwise, all you have is a "hireling" who worries more about days off, benefits, and vacations than the work in the vineyard.

We had so few junior highers that I was embarrassed when folks asked. I asked our elders to consider seeking out a person who had a burden for that intimidating age. If we could find such a person, we could pay a salary and ask him or her to go reach junior high kids. Carl Palmer was a single young man about to be married and he had a real love and burden for this age. In addition, he was about to graduate from a nearby Bible college. He was our man . . . and God's. At first he could take most of our group with him on his motorcycle. It soon proved too small so he bought a van. Within a few months we needed buses. Junior high kids were everywhere. They came mid-week for Bible study, dozens of them. Our vision had become reality, and all it took was to find a man with a burden, pay him enough to live on, and then raise it so he could get married and continue on.

Reason three: You believe God is leading you to take an unusual step. The "leading of the Lord" is always related to a burden on the heart of a believer. Some action needs to be taken to meet a particular need. Of the possibilities available, you finally select one, feeling in your heart that the step is the best one.

A verse I have noted in the back of my Bible to be used when "hearing" the voice of God is this one: "Whether you turn to the right or to the left, your ears will hear a voice behind you, saying, This is the way; walk in it" (Isaiah 30:21 NIV).

If you have heard the voice of God and you take steps to follow the direction you have received, the promise of scripture is that some definite confirmation will come. And the confirmation will not be some ambiguous or subjective experience. It will be the sure hand of the Lord doing what no human could contrive.

For years I had dreamed of adding a total sports ministry

to our church activities. Others shared the vision. My family's church in Santa Cruz had offered summer softball and winter volleyball. Someone with vision had led that church to build a recreation hall. These activities had helped to keep me in the church through the vital years of my teens. I know that other boys and girls, as well as sports-minded adults, could be reached for Christ through athletics or kept in the church when they might otherwise slip away.

We had thirteen acres and fine church and classroom facilities, but some of us looked longingly across our back fence at the pasture hillside next door. It could provide additional parking, a site for a future gymnasium, and a full soccer field and softball diamond. But we didn't own it. Our budget was strained to the limit as we had just relocated and remodeled. Our struggle for a use permit had been so fierce and expensive that the thought of applying for another permit was unwelcomed.

Still, we reasoned, if we don't own it, we will never be able to use the land as we desire. Maybe we could tie it up in some way, such as a lease with an option to buy or first right to purchase if it should one day be for sale. At least we ought to meet the owner and talk about our vision for the future.

Thus it was on March 3, 1975, that Tom Moore, our business manager, and I drove to Mr. Charles Kring's office in his shopping center a few miles away to talk about the property. It was our intention to explore the possibilities. Suddenly I felt "the leading of the Lord" to say something I hadn't planned to say. I blurted out, surprising all three of us with what I said, "Mr. Kring, you have more money than you will ever spend and more property than you will ever use. Why don't you give us some of your land that is adjacent to our church property? We need it for sports, youth work, and parking."

No one broke the silence. Mr. Kring pulled out file drawers, removed folders, maps, and other papers, spreading them out on his desk. He moved to the large map on his office wall and contemplated it for quite some time, still not saying anything. My hands perspired. Tom was very silent. Was it the "leading of the Lord" or a foolish request? Mr. Kring wasn't a member of our church, although we knew him to be favorable to us while we fought the battle of the use permit. At least he hadn't opposed us in the public hearings, and one day his wife had come in for a tour of our buildings and to ask some questions. These fine people love our country and believe in things that are right and pure and good.

When he sat down again, he looked right at me and asked a very direct question, "How much land?" My answer was even shorter, "Ten acres." I hadn't intended to ask him for a gift of land in the first place, so my answer to his question was without any forethought, although Tom and I had obviously gone to him to talk about "some land."

Mr. Kring, dignified gentleman that he is, looked at my face for a few moments, then stood up. We stood as well. "My wife is in Europe at the moment," he said. "I will mention your proposal to her when she returns. Thank you for stopping by." He smiled as he firmly shook our hands and walked us to the door.

"Tom," I said when back in his car, "I'm sorry. I hope he wasn't offended. I really had no intention of doing that." As we drove away, Tom said, as I recall, "Might as well ask. Who knows? Maybe it was the 'leading of the Lord.' Time will tell."

Well, time passed, weeks and months of time. One day a man came in and introduced himself as Mr. Kring's real estate representative. He had a proposition, the first of many we were to hear. We would buy eleven acres and Mr. Kring would give us four. We would receive a gift of some land in another town which we would sell and then buy the land we wanted. The months passed and nothing definite was ever settled on. Two years passed. The church was growing rapidly, but it looked as if the property item was too complicated ever to materialize.

Then one day in August, 1977, I received a letter with the Kring's address on the envelope. When I opened it, here is what I read:

Dear Reverend Rickard,

I have been made aware of your need of additional land for the use of your church.

It is my intent to make a gift to you of fifteen acres of land fronting Hicks Road adjoining your property on the south as shown on the enclosed plan. I understand you have an engineer that recently surveyed your boundary and is qualified to prepare the necessary parcel map . . .

Very truly yours,
Charles U. Kring

A gift of fifteen beautiful acres of land, ten of which were usable! Enough for soccer field, softball diamond, parking, a gym, plus some additional land to develop later! We could see it in our minds, and now it is reality. Four thousand people a year are involved in sporting activities of all kinds. Two full-time ministers of sports and recreation lead our program which includes outreach teams in city leagues, teams to send overseas, and a ministry to prisons through athletic competition. Saturdays now see hundreds of children involved in soccer or softball. Summer evenings resound with the crack of bat against ball and the sounds of teams intent on victory.

Some churches don't need a sports ministry or a junior high ministry or a ministry to seniors. If God places a burden on the pastor's heart, God has probably prepared a person to fulfill that need. All it takes is one year's salary and then that staff person's contribution is "free"! If he or she is effective, the people he draws into the church will soon be covering all costs of that ministry by the additional tithes and offerings.

Reason four: A proven, capable leader suddenly becomes available. This is rarely employed, yet it can prove to be the most effective of all. You ask him or her to join your staff, then you figure out what that leader's job description might be. Industry has long since discovered that some people are gifted leaders by nature and will be a great asset to the company wherever they are placed. When such a person is available, they employ him and then begin to determine how his talents can best benefit the operation.

A person called of God into ministry can specialize in any number of fields with great effectiveness.

At a certain point our elders came to the conviction that we needed help in the area of business management. The responsibility had become too large for the lay people upon whom it fell. Someone was needed to give full-time attention to all financial and business aspects of our church work.

The Lord knew our need and had prepared the man to fill it, a man who had the capacity to grow and assume even larger responsibilities. I have mentioned Tom Moore previously. We met at the suggestion of his daughter who was a member of our church. She said, "Dad is ready to take early retirement from Boy Scouts of America where he has been in administration for years." I agreed to meet him for lunch at what was once Jeff's Restaurant in Los Gatos. Before I left for the appointment, I jotted down a few major areas we needed to cover. We had no written job description yet.

I liked Tom immediately. He had once felt a real calling for the ministry but had accepted another worthy calling working with boys. More recently, at age 56, he had expressed a longing for full-time involvement in the Lord's work. With his wife's encouragement, Tom had decided to consider early retirement and to see if any doors were open. Our meeting was by divine appointment. The areas of our need were the very areas of his experience and expertise.

A pastor can't take the time to function as church administrator when facilities and employees increase, along with financial complexities. An administrator is needed with real skills in dealing with personnel, budgets, building projects, maintenance, and finances.

I believe that the Lord will send the laborers into the fields at the right moment. Our part is to be sensitive to the moment and to the person sent to us.

I cannot close this chapter without some mention of a problem which prevents many pastors from leading their churches beyond a certain point. This point is reached when they have to turn over major responsibilities to someone else. A growing church will need to have a staff. At first the staff is small and the role of the pastor isn't much different than before. However, if growth continues, eventually the pastor has to major on preaching and overall administration, letting others do weddings, funerals, conduct meetings, make most hospital calls, and do the counseling.

The difficult hurdle for a pastor to overcome is to allow staff members to become pastors to their areas of the church membership. If jealousy gains a foothold, staff changes will be frequent and unrest common.

The only way one man can be pastor to many hundreds or thousands is by delegating his responsibilities to others. He preaches, counsels, visits, teaches, and he leads, but much of the work with individuals, committees, and classes is in the hands of his staff. They become an extension of his ministry, although they feel as if their areas are their own. Their areas are indeed their own, but all of the areas together make up the whole. No one on the staff sees this viewpoint as clearly as the senior pastor.

A church cannot grow beyond a certain numerical point unless the pastor is able to delegate others to do many things that he would enjoy doing himself.

PRINCIPLES TO PONDER

1. There is no "best" order of adding staff.

2. The Lord leads by inner promptings.

3. The Lord confirms His leadings by the fruit of the action taken.

4. Successful delegation is essential to church growth.

5. "You have not because you ask not."

15

EFFECTIVE CHURCH LEADERSHIP

Five of us ordered our breakfasts and enjoyed cups of steaming hot coffee as we waited for our food to be brought. Someone jokingly said, "We had better not add any more ministers or we won't fit into this booth." Tuesday breakfast was our staff meeting, although we had no prepared agendas, no order of business, and no notes were taken.

In many ways this was a most enjoyable manner of leading and working together. And it was effective enough. We each knew everything that was happening in the church. The reasons for meeting were communication and uninterrupted fellowship on a regular basis. The leaders of any smaller church can do something similar, whether they are full time with the church or laymen.

As the church adds ministers, the same two basic principles must be followed: communication and fellowship in a team-like setting. When these are broken down into a practical application of church leadership, it means several things.

People need to be told what they are expected to accomplish. I had never seen a job description until our staff had grown to about seven full-time ministers. From his rich background in Scouting, Tom Moore suggested that we begin to prepare some kind of method of writing out what I expected of each staff person. He would do the same for custodians, secretaries, and any part-time help we required. (Included in Appendix A are job descriptions for three basic ministries.)

A job description should not be detailed nor complex. It should state in simple terms the major responsibilities and to whom the person is to give account.

People need to set personal goals which indicate their intentions and plans for fulfilling their job descriptions. These goals then become the vehicle for measuring the progress of a particular ministry.

People need to be free to fulfill their ministries in their own individual ways. If the pastor and the person in charge of an area of ministry agree on the goals, then the ministry will satisfy all concerned, as long as it is moving along the accepted direction. A pitfall to mark is in the category of methods. Not only must there be agreement on goals, but agreement on methods of reaching the goals.

People need regular staff meetings or team meetings to maintain a team spirit and to keep the line of communication open. No manager of a team, whether in the ministry or in secular business, is able to effectively manage more than five to seven others. The members of this team are equals in terms of responsibility, other than the main leader of the team. Being equals, they are able to come to group decisions, an excellent way of dealing with the subject of methods.

For example, if the minister of music or the lay person in charge felt that he might consider adding a new dimension to congregational worship, the staff meeting would be the place to explore the possibilities. Should we encourage or discourage applause after baptisms? Should we encourage clapping in rhythm to some singing? Might we take the offering at the close of the service instead of sooner? Is the raising of hands in praise acceptable in our way of worship?

Another example might concern the youth minister or sponsor who wants an opinion from the others. Should junior high youth have an annual all-night activity or is that for older youth only? Any suggestions for ministering to Christian high school students as opposed to public high school students? Or the business manager wants the others to discuss the problem of communication room set-up requirements to the custodians. How can we ease frustrations in building use? Who is responsible for kids who choose to skip services but hang around the halls?

The pastor says, "I need your opinion. Shall we invite so and so, who has written that he is available, to minister to our people in view of the fact that it will be right after Easter?"

And so the staff meetings go. A previously prepared agenda keeps them from becoming too lengthy or from rambling.

People need to know that their "boss" is aware of their work and approves. Individual, one-on-one meetings need to take place frequently between pastor and staff members. These may be carefully prepared, as in matters of great concern to either. They may be spontaneous, such as a lunch together or a quick "got a minute?" drop-in visit or a phone call.

Regular, planned staff meetings or team meeting and frequent visits build relations which tend to result in long ministries together.

The typical secular annual performance review hardly fits since ministers are not performing a function for which they get paid but are fulfilling the call of God to minister among His people. Even so, some method of determining effectiveness is necessary. If the pastor knows what he wants his team to be doing, it isn't hard to determine if they are doing it. Included in Appendix B is a form which has proven helpful for annual reviewing.

PRINCIPLES TO PONDER

1. Every responsible position in the church needs to be described in simple form on paper.

2. Limitations of responsibility and extent of authority need to be carefully spelled out.

3. A servant can't serve well if he doesn't know what he is supposed to do and when he has accomplished it.

16.

WELCOMING IN NEW MEMBERS

We sat in a comfortable room, the five of us ministers on our church staff. It was a relaxed discussion, but all of us were very alert and interested. The subject was, "How can we do a better job of bringing new members into the mainstream of our church?"

To gain membership was easy. People either transferred in as immersed believers from some other church or they automatically became members following their conversion and baptism.

We believe in local church membership. Unless people say in some manner, "We're with you in the essentials of faith, and we want to help you reach our area for Christ," we can't really ask them to take responsibility. We often encourage believers who have no local church fellowship where they are active for Christ to join our fellowship and to serve with all their hearts. It is also scriptural to add to the church day by day those that are being saved. But then what? How will the new ones learn what we expect of them in our fellowship? How will we determine who is mature enough to assume personal responsibility?

Our "old way" was to prepare New Member packets

with various tracts, by-laws, materials, and schedules inside and ask deacons and elders to deliver them. Unfortunately, this was never a glowing success. Many packets never got delivered as planned. Some were merely handed over at church with a "Let's get together one of these days." I am afraid that some of those packets slid around in the trunks of cars until they fell apart!

Then we tried another plan. We invited new members over a certain period of time to come to a specific evening service. They were invited to the front where we introduced each one and then handed them their packet plus a new Bible. After church we had a time of refreshments during which the kids grabbed all the cookies and the rest of us met new members.

Our discussion had reviewed all of this, with a few laughs. Finally I asked, "Well, just what is it that we really want to do?" Someone said, "They need to know what they believe. We have to ground them in the Word on the basic doctrines." Another said, "But not all of them need that. Some could probably teach it. After all, one in four comes to us already a Christian, and some of them are mature believers. Some have been teachers, deacons, and even ministers." The discussion continued. "Wait a minute, I think they need to be warmly welcomed and made to feel loved and wanted, first of all. Why does it have to be so heavy and serious?" "Why not a special class at a convenient hour just for new members?" "I'll bet some others would want to take it who have been with us less than a year." "What subjects will we cover?"

"Who will teach it?" I said, "I think it ought to be led by one of us." Sudden silence as we all looked each other over. Everyone was already teaching at least one class except Tom Moore and me. I was preaching four times each Sunday, three times in the morning and once at 7:00 P.M.

All eyes fastened on Tom. "Why don't Isabel and I take on the new members' class?" he offered, as we all broke up in laughter. Then Tom offered a new thought. "Why not run a continuous class which never ends. Just graduate out each week those who have completed the six subjects and bring in the adult new members who are brand new?" Someone said, "Great idea! That way we can invite people who were baptized the Sunday before and transfers who just came into membership."

Eventually, six subjects were defined. Different staff people and lay people would cover the various subjects. Tom and Isabel would be host and hostess and always be there. Introductions, name tags, coffee, "graduation," and developing a congenial, relaxed atmosphere would be their responsibility. A secretary would have added to her job description the task of personally inviting, almost insisting, the new members to the class. A letter would follow, with time, place, and a further word of warm welcome.

The first six subjects were as follows:

Music/Youth
Elders/Board
Missions
Adult Ministries/Women's Ministries
Preschool-Elementary
Stewardship

Eventually the number of sessions was extended to nine weeks, as at present, adding these subjects:

Day School/Sports
Spiritual Gifts
Shepherding

These classes were for the purpose of acquainting our new members with our church methods or philosophy on the various subjects. We discovered that we had developed a definite point of view on youth work. For example, we build our whole youth ministry on the Word of God and discipleship and have strong convictions about the use of rock music or gimmickery to get a crowd. And music. We want servants who sing, not soloists who want to be seen and heard.

Church government, the faith promise approach to missions, our no pressure method of trusting God to supply our financial needs—all of these topics needed to be understood by our new members. We believe that this plan for the process of assimilating new members from diverse backgrounds has contributed greatly to unity of purpose in our total membership.

A secondary purpose was almost a byproduct of the major purpose, and that was to provide a means of drawing the mature, newer members into an effective place of service.

New members need to feel like they are a part of the church. We could think of no better way to accomplish this than such a class. We assumed that each one desired to know as much as possible about the church. But, even more, they needed to know others. Thus the weekly activity of introducing the newest members of the class and those graduating out became of great value. In addition we introduced each person weekly. As a new member heard the name of each person up to nine times, (in his nine weeks in the class) he grew to know them. He was no longer a stranger. As he went to services, he could see several whose names he knew and who could greet him by name.

Each week we assured the roomful of comfortable people that we wanted to help them grow to Christian maturity, but they had to supply the commitment. Nearly all of them responded with enthusiasm. They could sense and see that we loved them and cared. In a warm setting, even those who might have remained on the fringes were drawn along farther than they had originally intended. Such a new members class is essential for building new people into the church.

PRINCIPLES TO PONDER:

1. New members need to be added to the fellowship of a local church in some definite way.

2. Many new members will respond eagerly to leaders who plan for their growth.

17

BUILDING UP NEW MEMBERS

Rain dripped steadily. Inside, the room was warm and the coffee was fragrant and hot. The subject was once again new members.

"We need more than a six-week class. Some of them know the Lord, but they don't know much more than that! They need some basic knowledge of the Word."

"Are they continuing on in a Sunday school class?" "Most are. We encourage them to continue to come at the hour of our new members class but to find an adult class. We give them a schedule."

"Our statistics keep going up. Attendance in the adult department is keeping pace. Why don't we offer another six-week class on 'Basics in Christian Doctrine,' and encourage all new Christians to take it, following their graduation from new members?"

I asked, "What subjects?" He had thought it out. "How to share your faith. Assurance of salvation. The ministry of the Holy Spirit." He named some other subjects.

"Great! But I don't like that class title. 'Basics in Doctrine' sounds too heavy, even though it really isn't. Why not call it . . ." He tapered off, unsure of a better title.

Another picked up on it, "How about 'Basics in Christian Living'?" We all yelled, "That's it!"

The subjects of that original class were as follows:
    Assurance of Salvation
    Forgiveness of Sin
    The Spirit-Filled Life
    Uniqueness of the Bible
    Overview of the Old Testament
    Overview of the New Testament

Two more ideas emerged which proved to be of great value in assimilating new members.

Tom Moore brought up both of them, again assisted by remarks, humor, and eventually definite plans from the others of us. "The new members need to meet you and Joyce," he said, in response to my lament that we felt we had no good means of meeting them. "Why don't you invite them to your home in groups of whatever your living room will hold?" He said, "We'll hold that out as an inducement to complete all six sessions. Let's call it something like 'Dessert with the Pastor.'" Further refinements included the same kinds of pies each time, purchased at the expense of the church and brought to our house by the Moores, who always helped us host the event. My wife prepared the coffee and punch, assisted by my secretary. Incidentally, we discovered that people preferred cream pies to fruit pies and that they didn't drink much coffee in hot weather!

The "Desserts with the Pastor" occurred about every four weeks, sometimes more often, usually on Thursday evenings. My wife maintains a rather orderly home at all times, a home furnished in antiques. She has never let entertaining become a difficult ordeal. We would rather call it "hospitality." Many an evening we were finishing the dinner dishes and moving chairs as the guests began to arrive! Paper plates and cups simplified things.

Tom Moore, acquainted with the new members through the new members class, welcomed the people, each one wearing a name tag. Then he introduced me. I carried a stool or small chair to a strategic place where I could see everyone and began the evening.

"We're glad to welcome you to our home and are honored that you took the time to come. And we're thrilled to have you in our church family. Let's just take a few minutes to meet each one. Could I start with you, Mr. and Mrs. Spangler? Have you been Christians long? When did it happen?" I would ask, "Tell me about your family" or, "What is your occupation?" "How did you find Los Gatos Christian Church?"

By the time we heard from thirty to forty people, it was a good time to break for dessert, then we reassembled. Seated again, Tom said, "Now it's your turn. Ask our pastor whatever you want to know about his family, his background, the church, how to refinish antiques or whatever you want to ask. Now who has the first question?"

It was usually, "How did you and Joyce meet?" Or it might be, "Where did you go to school?" or, "How often do you have these desserts?" Then the questions would began to fly. Keeping track of the time, I always led to a close, often joining our hands for prayer, by 9:30 or 9:45 P.M. Usually some lingered on to help us clean up and to ask questions which they hadn't wanted to voice in front of the whole group.

The second idea has also proved to be worth continuing. A new member dinner is held about six times a year to which the most recent new members are invited. We try to confirm each reservation so that the right number of tables is set up, although there is no cost to those attending. Usually the menu is a roast beef dinner, complete with dessert, prepared by one of our kitchen teams.

A new members dinner committee hosts the event, sitting with the guests, along with staff and elders. After dinner, we clear the tables and have each member introduce himself and those with him or her and tell where they work.

Our slide show contains the history of our church, an introduction of all staff by pictures, and then includes a little idea of our future vision, dreams, and plans. The new members always applaud this interesting portion. As pastor, I talk to them informally and extemporaneously for a few minutes at the end, challenging them to grow in commitment, knowledge, service, and stewardship. Usually, I tell the story of the "Miracle of Financing," chapter 10 of this book.

We in leadership feel that our efforts to draw new members in and our challenge to them to move ahead in their walk with the Lord is worth every effort.

PRINCIPLES TO PONDER:

1. A church that isn't taking in new members is dying.

2. To ignore new members is a sin.

18.

STARTING A CHURCH

I picked up the phone and called the young minister. "Rich, is the rumor true?" "Yes," he said, "Unfortunately, it is true. I am now among the unemployed." I said, "Tell me about it." And so the story came out. I had spent some time with him over a period of a few years. He liked what we were doing and the way we were doing it, and I had tried to guide him a little. Now it was over, although attendance had never been better. Often his church totaled well over 1000, and he had built a fine staff. The issue was a matter of doctrine: baptism. The elders saw it one way and Rich saw it another . . . and they did the hiring and firing! "But Rich," I said, "Can't you find enough common ground on which to stand together? The Lord is blessing so well and the church seems to be doing great." "No, " he said, "It is deeper than the final issue. It is a matter of who leads the church. I could split the church, but I don't want to." "What will you do?" was my question while I stalled for time. My heart was increasing its tempo. I knew what I wanted to say, and out it came. "Rich, come to Los Gatos and serve for a couple of years on our staff. Help me with the preaching. We'll figure out a job description. You and Wilma need time to think and to feel good about the ministry again." I couldn't stop. For years the plan had been on my heart. The final key was ready to drop into place. "Rich, in two years we'll start a new church with several hundred of our best members. You and Wilma will be ready to go by then. What do you say?"

I could hardly wait for his phone call, praying for the Lord to move him to join us. We had grown to the point of needing four morning services each Sunday and two evening services. Others helped with preaching, but they had heavy responsibilities. I felt an obligation to preach four of the six sermons each week, but not six. I needed help! We had auditorium plans in the works, but no immediate relief. The best we could hope for was about two years.

From the time our church had reached an average attendance of five hundred, some people expressed an interest in church planting. The years rolled by and the idea was always in the back of my mind. New buildings, additional services, and even a major relocation move occupied a higher priority. When we met for planning sessions, we always talked about the time to come when we would start a new church. Meanwhile attendances rose past 1000, past 2000, and well into the 3000's for morning worship.

We were familiar with several ways new churches get started . . . a few families rent a building . . . a denomination sends a man . . . a church splits . . . a church sends out 50-150 people to a small piece of property and a first unit building . . . an ethnic group holds Sunday afternoon services . . . cultural changes result in relocation, with a remnant left in the former facilities.

But in our case, none of these ways seemed to fit the need. People came to Los Gatos Christian because of the advantages of a large church ministry, such as specialized children's work and youth work, many choirs, and in our case, verse-by-verse expository sermons through Bible books, and a highly developed shepherding ministry.

We had divided our entire membership into more than fifty neighborhood shepherding fellowships, meeting monthly for a potluck supper in the various geographical areas for the purpose of building relationships and edification. To our surprise, some of the shepherding groups which were located quite some distance from our church facilities were among our largest and strongest. In fact, in view of the strength of several such groups from certain areas, a new church for such people had to be considered.

Just the previous summer, in August of 1976, at an all-day elder/staff planning session, we had put "starting a new church" at the top of our priority list for 1977. We even detailed how we wanted to do it. Five hundred to one thousand members would be the "nucleus." At least a staff of four would be needed. The pastor, whoever it was that the Lord would send, would need to be committed to expository preaching. A large facility would be needed, near a freeway or two. The new church should have a choir or two already functioning before the first Sunday. We even figured out a tentative budget.

As I looked around the tables at the thirty men in that meeting, it suddenly dawned on me that some of these very men and some of my own fine staff would no doubt go with the new church. A surge of emotion threatened to surface. No one saw me look quickly away and blink back the evidence.

Now we were really going to do it! Rich and Wilma Marshall joined us on September 6, 1977. He began to preach with me through the Gospel of Mark. The outline sheet, included in our bulletin, was the same for each service, but we prepared our sermons separately, of course.

And it worked! People liked him. When the two of them sang together, hearts were melted. We didn't say much that first year to the congregation, but elders and staff began the countdown.

Which staff would go? Which board members? The Lord began to impress them one by one. One of our youth ministers felt the burden to go. One of our Christian education ministers said, "We think we ought to go, if 'they' want us." So far there was no "they" to hire anyone! A music intern wanted to be considered.

Our new auditorium seating 2000 was being built. By January, 1979, we were in it for three morning services and one jam packed evening service. People had to stand when the extra chairs were filled. But what a dilemma! Back to double evening services? We couldn't bear the thought.

Thus, on February 11, 1979, an alternate evening service began in a rented gymnasium of a Bible college located fifteen miles from Los Gatos Christian Church. Rich Marshall continued the evening series of Bible messages through the Book of Revelation on the same schedule I was on. Seven hundred fourteen people met for that first evening. A choir had been formed and sang well, memorizing their music as they had at L.G.C.C. In spite of a warm California spring and increasing summer heat, that weekly evening meeting averaged in the 600's.

Momentum was increasing, and plans were laid for a date to begin Sunday morning services. September 9, 1979, would be the date, exactly two years from the Sunday the Marshalls had joined our team. Five hundred seventy-eight came for Sunday school and 742 met for worship. A board was formed, all formerly members of our church. A definite budget was established, although for one year all of their funds would be handled in our business office and by our business manager. The church was now in operation, but in rented facilities that were inadequate.

The rumor had been around a long time that Bethel Church, Assembly of God, had property and planned to build and relocate. Now, in God's own timing, they began . . . and we began to seriously consider buying their fine facility. The location was perfect, the price was $1.5 million, and they wanted to sell. So, while we were building a new $2 million dollar auditorium, we now faced the prospect of buying a $1.5 million dollar building for the new congregation. They would also participate, of course. Debenture notes were sold to both congregations; all $1.5 million sold in three months.

Crossroads Bible Church is now a strong healthy church, with attendance often exceeding 2000. The new baby church has bought their $1.5 million dollar building complex from us. This amounts to a transfer of responsibility for the debt from Los Gatos Christian to Crossroads Bible Church.

For one year we operated with two church boards, but with our business manager serving on both of them since we had determined that a single budget was best. This arrangement proved to be effective and practical. Two points of view emerged, interestingly enough. The new church wanted their full independence sooner than one year. Los Gatos Christian Church would have preferred to maintain full direction somewhat longer than one year.

Where did we make mistakes in all of this? We made no planning errors. But there certainly was real pain in giving birth to this big baby! The first week of their full-fledged all-day church schedule produced an unexpected emotional impact on me as pastor. I actually went into a private room and wept. I rejoiced at their success and because of our vitality to do such a thing, but still I wept.

Those seven hundred who left us to pioneer included many families which had been with us for years. I had prayed with some of those men, had met with some until the wee hours on various matters, had laid plans of faith, had suffered through setbacks and trials, and I just could hardly stand to see them go. Yet their very willingness to leave, in order to start a new church, was a personal satisfaction to me. Like parents who approve of their daughter's or son's choice in marriage, yet weep at the wedding, I had to do that very thing. For this, in all the planning and dreaming of a new church, I was totally unprepared.

Nor were we fully prepared to give up so many of those people from evening church or from places of responsible service. We absorbed the financial loss easily enough, though not so easily as not to feel it. We felt it. It was mature, wise people, dependable in service, and their word of faith and encouragement that we missed, and still miss. Sometimes I get a lump in my throat when I see them at a wedding or at some Christian event and long a bit for "the good old days."

PRINCIPLES TO PONDER:

1. Proven leadership for new churches is vital for success.

2. Plan the work and then work the plan.

3. Large churches should consider starting a church.

19

THE ROAD AHEAD

Present attendances for the three morning services at Los Gatos Christian usually exceed 4000. The warm, song-filled evening services are attended by more than 2000, of which half are under thirty. Of the young people, including many young married couples, more than two hundred are committed to full-time career Christian service, especially cross-cultural missionary work, as the Lord opens doors. The responsibility of sending these people to the nations of the world is not taken lightly by the congregation. The present 1.3 million dollars for missions annually will not be nearly enough. That figure will need to be doubled and more.

The leaders of Los Gatos Christian Church are constantly asking, seeking, and knocking to find ways of advancing the Gospel of Christ through the ministry of their local church. If God wants to open the doors of space and finances to minister to 10,000 people, they are not frightened by the possibility. If television is the best way to get the message of Christ to the area, they are willing to face the extreme costs of purchasing time on major stations.

The church is indeed a living organism which will grow

in numbers, influence, and effectiveness if the obstacles are removed.

Church planting has become a major goal, whether done on a large scale, such as Crossroads Bible Church, or on a smaller scale. Plans are presently set to add growth-minded churches regularly. Crossroads Church is currently starting a new church several miles from their property.

Another objective of the leaders of Los Gatos Christian Church is to take a public stand on moral issues, to be the conscience of the community, along with other Bible churches. Weekly television broadcasts reach into the homes of multitudes, including San Francisco, a city that has never experienced a spiritual awakening. With the media largely controlled by the secular humanists, television time gives our church a direct voice to the people. Many are listening. Week after week people are coming to Christ and into the church as a result. Almost every Sunday someone is baptized in our services who was reached through T.V.

We are experiencing an increasing burden to live out the unity of the Body of Christ in our relationships with other churches. Organizational unity is not desirable, doctrinal unity is not likely, ecumenical unity is not scriptural (as proposed by the liberal denominations), but a recognition of the essential unity of the church is both possible and practical. Our local church leaders have a great desire to simply love the people of Christ, whoever and wherever they are. We need each other. We belong to each other.

As time has passed, we have found ourselves looked to by some as the means of information and help in solving church growth problems. The principles in this book have been learned in the crucible of experience, not always under pleasant circumstances. We think that others could apply them less painfully than we did, if they understood better than we did just what to expect. We love the church, church leaders, and the people of God everywhere. We are in competition only against Satan and the powers of darkness. If this book proves to be helpful it has served the author's purposes and that of Multnomah Press.

APPENDIX A
CALLING A STAFF PERSON

Selection of capable people to fill positions on church staffs is of tremendous importance. If you get the right people, the work prospers. If you make wrong choices, problems multiply. It is easier to hire than to fire. Everything hinges on leadership.

We sometimes desire so strongly to fill a particular ministry that our eagerness overcomes our judgment. We want someone to be the "right" one so much that we gloss over warning signs. We push them out of our minds for the moment, assuring ourselves that "we can live with that" or "we will change him later."

I well remember calling a person to fill a key spot on our staff. Obviously, for the sake of feelings and reputations, I must be very general here. We made our decision, ignoring the clues we should have considered, but it was the wrong choice. It didn't take long to realize it, just a few weeks. What do you do? In our case we faced our wrong selection, admitted it, apologized for it, and freed that person from all responsibilities . . . but we paid a good salary for an entire year. We actually paid a person not to work for us. Out of that experience we developed a plan for adding all staff people.

When we see a need that no longer can be adequately filled by members of our congregation, due to time and skills required, a job description is carefully worked out. Pre-interview forms are sent to prospective staff people. From the information obtained, interviews may or may not be scheduled. If an interview is scheduled, the information on the forms becomes the focus of the personnel committee, a group of several elders, as they meet with the candidate. (They will make a final recommendation to the council of elders.)

God doesn't call a man or woman to a ministry without also calling the wife or husband as well, since they are "one flesh." Therefore, we call a couple to a staff position, not just the man or woman. We want as much commitment from the spouse as from the person we are technically considering.

The following material may be copied and changed as required to aid church leaders in making good selections for the work of the ministry.

PRE-INTERVIEW FORM
DOCTRINE

Name _____

Date _____

DOCTRINAL SURVEY

1. Who is Jesus Christ according to your understanding?

2. What did His death accomplish?

3. What is the significance of the resurrection?

4. Who is the Holy Spirit?

5. How does a person become a Christian?

6. What is the basis for forgiveness for sins committed after receiving Christ?

7. Where are believers who have died?

8. What is your view of the inspiration of the Bible?

9. What do you feel about "tongues"?

10. Would you be willing to refrain from teaching doctrines unique to your denomination or background, but which are not common to the body of Christ?

11. Do you have freedom in working with people from all denominational backgrounds?

12. Could you work in a totally nondenominational atmosphere with no allegiances to man-made brotherhoods or fellowships?

PRE-INTERVIEW FORM
PERSONAL

Name _____ Age _____
Address _____
City/State/Zip _____ Phone (___) _____
Spouse's Name _____ Age _____
Children's Names and Ages _____

CONVERSION AND EXPERIENCE:
1. When and where did you become a Christian?

    Your spouse?

2. What training and experience have you had for the area of service considered?

3. What is your spouse's attitude toward this ministry?

4. Are your children involved Christians?

5. What kind of home did you come from?

    Spouse?

6. What are your strong points?

   Weak points?

7. What leisure time interests do you have?

8. Do you feel that you can work well in a multiple-staff ministry?

9. Do you have questions you wish for us to answer before taking the time and effort to come to Los Gatos for an interview?

10. Please include a picture of yourself when returning the pre-interview forms.

APPENDIX B
GIVING LEADERSHIP DIRECTION

We assume too much in church leadership. We employ or call someone for a particular responsibility and then fail to tell him exactly what it is we want him to do and how he will know when he has accomplished it.

Just as in the business world and in the field of industry specialization is the norm, so it is becoming in church work. Church leaders call a man to do youth work or to be youth minister, but they fail to tell him to whom he reports, what his limits of authority are, and what he is to accomplish.

Why not job descriptions and ministry reviews? Before a person is hired by the church leaders to fill a staff position, the work is defined and laid out clearly. Interviews can and should zero in on the job description and the applicant's potential for accomplishing it. Reviews should be given so the staff person knows how he is performing. On the following pages, three basic job descriptions and a ministry review form are reproduced. Feel free to copy them, change them, and use them. They can also serve as a model for preparing additional job descriptions and reviews. One thing to keep in mind is that no person ever fits into a position without some adjustments and change. Therefore, be prepared to re-write each job description after about one year. The needs change, people grow and change, and the job changes.

STAFF POSITION
DESCRIPTION

Title: Minister of Christian Education
Position Reports to: Senior pastor
Date of Employment:
Incumbent:
Date Prepared:

POSITION CONCEPT:

The Minister of Christian Education shall serve as a part
of the pastoral staff. As a member of that staff he shall provide leadership in all Christian education programs exclusive of the pulpit ministries as follows:

1. To develop and implement a strategy for bringing our
   members and constituents to full Christian maturity.
   By that it is meant:
   a. A knowledge of the Word.
   b. A disciplined walk.
   c. The ability to share Christ with others.
   d. To evidence the fruit of the Spirit.
   e. To understand spiritual gifts and learn to use them.
2. To give counsel and leadership to our Christian education staff as they lead our Sunday school, week-day
   activities including Bible Institute, home Bible
   studies, camp ministries, scouting, and daily vacation Bible school.

PRINCIPLE DUTIES AND RESPONSIBILITIES:

1. Coordinate all instruction in the Sunday school de-
   partments (infant through senior citizens). Junior

high, high school, college are under youth department.

2. Is responsible for coordinating all room assignments and building utilization exclusive of the church auditorium.

3. Is responsible for continuous appraisal of the curriculum.

4. Plans, organizes and administers the teacher/staff inservice training programs throughout the church body.

5. Is responsible for new teacher recruitment and training.

6. Supervises and coordinates a Bible Institute program.

7. Supervises and coordinates all weekly Christian education activities including home Bible studies, scouting, coaches clinic, women's fellowship and other religious instruction carried on during the week.

8. Is responsible for supervising and coordinating all summer camps ministries and daily vacation Bible school (excluding junior high, college, careers and sports camps).

9. Coordinates and directs the library and book store program of the church.

10. Develop and monitor an acceptable record keeping program for the Sunday school.

11. Meet and consult with the Christian education committee of the church and regularly report all activities and concerns of the program.

12. Coordinate the religious instruction of the Christian day school with the other Christian education activities of the church.

13. Perform such other duties as may be assigned by the senior pastor.

STAFF RELATIONSHIPS:

1. Recognize the importance of good relationship with the entire staff, their families, and all other church employees.
2. Work in harmony with all church policies.
3. Give leadership and supervision to all ministers and any other paid staff who are to report to the minister of Christian education.
4. Meet regularly with our Christian education staff for the purpose of helping them fulfill their ministry.

RESPONSIBILITIES TO CONGREGATIONAL LEADERS:

1. Attend elders meetings and board meetings.
2. Develop a team of members, including at least one elder and more than one deacon to assist in this ministry.

STAFF POSITION
DESCRIPTION

Title: Minister of Business Administration
Position Reports to: Senior pastor
Date of Employment:
Incumbent:
Date Prepared:

POSITION CONCEPT:

Serve as minister responsible for the business administration of the church, including:

1. Acquisition of property.
2. Expansion and development of church properties.
3. Financial planning and management.
4. Office management, property management, and related responsibilities.
5. Personnel, other than ministerial.

PRINCIPAL RESPONSIBILITIES:

1. Coordinate construction of new facilities with architect, engineers, and contractors, as well as municipal and jurisdictional authorities. Work with necessary church bodies in developing plans for the continuing expansion of the church.
2. Pursue the acquisition of school and other properties.
3. Supervise and approve renovations and improvements to existing facilities.
4. Organize and direct the sacrificial giving program.
5. Establish a deferred giving and wills program.
6. Coordinate legal matters of the church.
7. Coordinate the development of all loan programs.

8. Coordinate insurance programs, including employee health and medical plan, church liability, fire, theft, and vehicle policies.
9. Employee relations, including maintaining employee files, preparation of letters of employment and job descriptions. Coordinate employee benefits program.
10. Budget management.
11. Purchasing—sources and control.
12. Tape ministry.
13. Coordination of audit—internal and external.
14. Equipment inventory.
15. Kitchen management.
16. Keep congregation informed.
17. Establish capital budget and approve expenditures against it.
18. Serve on finance committee.
19. Serve on building committee.
20. Advise on salary increments.
21. Develop long-range plans with proper committees related to projected growth.

SPECIAL RESPONSIBILITIES:
1. Coordinate new members' class.
2. Participate in church Business Administrators Association.
3. Community relations.

STAFF POSITION
DESCRIPTION

Title: Minister of Missions
Position Reports to: Senior pastor
Date of Employment:
Incumbent:
Date Prepared:

POSITION CONCEPT:

The minister of missions has basically a three-fold function:

1. To continually develop within the church an ongoing program of communication to the membership the knowledge of, and the burden for, what God is doing worldwide. This program is to involve the church in a tangible, effective, and practical way through support of efforts to communicate the gospel, disciple the nations, and plant the Church beyond the local church's normal circle of opportunity.

2. To be knowledgeable through research, training, and investigation as to what God is doing the world over pertaining to the status and strategy of world evangelization.

3. To function as a team member of the local church staff, bearing responsibility for the nurture and discipleship of the membership.

PRINCIPAL RESPONSIBILITIES:

1. Implement a total missions program in accordance with the general missions policy.

2. Maintain a high level of missiology expertise. Keep

informed through research, field visits, and special study of mission agencies, so as to be able to recommend support for personnel and projects that are effective in reaching the world with the gospel.

3. Leadership of the Missions Committee
   a. Provide long-term continuity to the missions program.
   b. Recommend the appointment of members to the committee (with approval of elders).
   c. Inaugurate subcommittees as required to accomplish the general missions program. Appoint subcommittee chairmen.
   d. Assure the education of the committee members as pertains to general missiology, the world situation, and the status of the church's worldwide ministry.
   e. Provide for spiritual guidance of the committee in concert with the missions elder.
4. Keep missions before the church membership through reports, missions education, special speakers, and information regarding worldwide outreach and needs.
5. Prepare and take responsibility for the annual Faith Promise Missions Conference, including selection and approval of program and speakers.
6. Provide counsel for church members that are potential candidates for missionary service.

SPECIAL RESPONSIBILITIES:
1. Supervise and train (disciple) missions interns.
2. Supervise missions secretary.
3. Administer a short term missionary program.
4. Prepare mission articles and input to the Newsette and other church publications.

5. Select and/or approve special missions speakers.
6. Represent the missions program to the church board, including presentation of missions recommendations for their approval.
7. Encourage in whatever way possible the development of missions outreach in other churches.
8. Local church responsibilities as assigned by senior pastor.

MINISTRY REVIEW

Employee Name _____

Department _____

Position Title _____

Current Position Starting Date_____

A. Rate on a scale of 1 to 10; 10 being the highest level.

_____ 1. Leads his department effectively.

_____ 2. Shows evidence of constant reading and study of the Word and related material.

_____ 3. When called upon to speak publicly, has his message well-prepared.

_____ 4. His public speaking is clear and motivating.

_____ 5. He has a heart for the people's needs.

_____ 6. He works well in co-operation with me.

_____ 7. He keeps me informed through written reports.

_____ 8. He keeps me informed verbally.

_____ 9. There is good evidence that his counseling load is in proportion to other duties and is effective.

_____ 10. He has a burden for the unsaved and regularly shares his faith.

_____ 11. He shows concern for the world-wide mission of the church.

_____ 12. He is effective in discipling others to assume some of his ministry, especially in training counselors for women.

_____ 13. He develops creative plans for increasing his effectiveness by stimulating others to serve the Lord.

_____ 14. His home is in constant use for the Lord.

_____ 15. His wife is fully supportive of his ministry.

_____ 16. He is available for hospital calls and emergency situations.

_____ 17. His children show evidence of commitment to Christ.

_____ 18. He is more effective as a minister at L.G.C.C. this year than last year.

_____ 19. He sets goals to be reached and gives a regular accounting.

_____ 20. Is his life characterized by the fruit of the Holy Spirit?

B. What is the position supposed to accomplish?

C. What process is being made toward fulfillment of the job description?

D. Should the job description be revised to suit the strengths and weaknesses of this minister?

E. Are there areas of improvement in order to do a better job?

F. Is the minister happy and fulfilled doing what he does?

G. Is the reviewer satisfied with what is being accomplished by the minister?

H. Are there new goals to be reached by this time next year?

I. Overall summary and recommendations.

J. Additional comments.

Minister's Signature _____ Date _____

Employee's Signature _____ Date _____

Review by _____ Date _____